THE CONTRIVED CORRIDOR

The Contrived Corridor

History and Fatality in Modern Literature

———

Harvey Gross

Ann Arbor
The University of Michigan Press

TO
AUSTIN WARREN
master teacher, beloved friend

Acknowledgments

Acknowledgments are made to the following publishers and agents for permission to use copyrighted materials:

To Harcourt Brace Jovanovich, Inc. and Faber and Faber Ltd for T. S. Eliot, *Collected Poems 1909–1962*, copyright 1936 by Harcourt Brace Jovanovich, Inc.; copyright © 1963, 1964 by T. S. Eliot. Reprinted by permission of the publishers.

To Harcourt Brace Jovanovich, Inc. for Robert Penn Warren's *All the King's Men*, copyright 1946 by Harcourt, Brace and Company, Inc.

To Holt, Rinehart and Winston, Inc. and Hamish Hamilton Ltd for André Malraux *Anti-Memoirs* copyright © 1967 by André Malraux; © 1968 by Holt, Rinehart and Winston, Inc. and Hamish Hamilton Ltd.

To Houghton, Mifflin Company for *Letters of Henry Adams, 1858–1891, 1892–1918*, copyright 1930, 1938 by Worthington C. Ford.

To Alfred A. Knopf, Inc. and S. Fischer Verlag G.m.b.H. (Frankfurt am Main) for excerpts from the following works of Thomas Mann:

Die Entstehung des Doktor Faustus © Bermann-Fischer Verlag Amsterdam, 1949.

The Story of a Novel, copyright © 1961 by Alfred A. Knopf, Inc.

Beim Propheten and *Der Tod in Venedig* from *Erzählungen* Stockholmer Gesamtausgabe, © Katharina Mann, 1958. "At the Prophet's and "Death in Venice" from *Stories of Three Decades*, copyright 1930, 1931, 1935, 1936 by Alfred A. Knopf, Inc.

Doktor Faustus © Thomas Mann, 1947.

To Random House, Inc., and Hamish Hamilton (London) for André Malraux, *Man's Hope*. Copyright 1937 Random House, Inc.; copyright © 1968 André Malraux.

To Random House, Inc., for André Malraux *The Temptation of the West* © 1926 by Random House, Inc.

To Random House, Inc. for Robert Penn Warren *You, Emperors, and Others*, © copyright 1958, 1959, 1960 by Robert Penn Warren.

Preface

This book makes a particular claim. Certain works forming our modernist heritage may be interpreted as a body of prophetic knowledge. This knowledge, revealed through myth, metaphor, and literary "fiction," expresses a heightened consciousness of history. While this claim drops a unifying thread through the six studies of individual writers, I try not to cut the cloth of my argument to a close-fitting pattern. Prophecy makes a traditional connection between literature and the deepest human concerns; I would hope my excursions into matters of general literary and cultural interest do not constitute digressions but rather developments of the essential humanity implicit in my theme.

My intellectual debts are many. I try to acknowledge specific borrowings in the notes; but since this study was conceived nearly twenty years ago, I have assimilated, through reading, conversation, and listening, a large number of ideas whose exact origins are no longer clear even to myself. Let me name some of the writers who can obviously be felt in the following pages. Hegel and Nietzsche represent adversary positions, the arch-historicist facing the arch-enemy of historicism. Like other great ideological antagonists of the nineteenth century (Wagner and Brahms, for example), they represent two diverging branches from the same Romantic trunk. Among recent writers on the history of ideas and the theory of history, I owe much to the work of Karl Löwith, especially to his *Meaning in History* and *From Hegel to Nietzsche;* and to the work of Hannah Arendt, especially to her *Between Past and Future*. I also found much stimulation in Frank Kermode's fascinating *The Sense of an Ending*.

I wish to thank friends who kindly read portions of the manuscript. Beatrice Gottlieb, Mary Goens, Frank Lentricchia, and Myron Simon offered suggestions which have improved the strength of my argument and the felicity of its expression. I owe special thanks to Elisabeth Case who encouraged me to work on this study during these years of disheartening political upheaval. My wife, Virginia La Rue Gross, has read the manuscript with her fine sense of style and pulled me out of numerous quagmires of illogic and jargon.

During the writing of this study, I have had gratifying institutional support. I received grants from the American Council of Learned Societies and The Rockefeller Foundation which allowed me a year of uninterrupted work. The Humanities Institute of the University of California; the Research Committee of the School of Humanities, and the Department of English and Comparative Literature of the University of California, Irvine, have all been generous with money for travel, research, and typing. I also wish to thank the Houghton Library of Harvard University for allowing me to examine books from T. S. Eliot's personal library.

Earlier versions of this study have appeared in the following periodicals: *PMLA, The Bucknell Review, The Centennial Review,* and *The University of Denver Quarterly.*

Newport Beach, California   H. G.
January 9, 1971

Contents

I   The Meaning of History, What *History* Means   1

I I   Henry Adams   20

I I I   T.S. Eliot   32

Geronton   32

The Waste Land   44

Four Quartets   58

I V   W.B. Yeats   74

V   The *Cantos* of Ezra Pound   100

V I   André Malraux   124

V I I   Thomas Mann   155

Afterword   185

Notes   191

Index   199

History has many cunning passages,
contrived corridors . . .
—T. S. Eliot, *Gerontion*

Necessity is not a fact but an interpretation.
—Friedrich Nietzsche,
The Will to Power

I

The Meaning of History,
What History *Means*

But the depths of history, which are continually at work to
rejuvenate creation, are in league with the prophets.
                                     —Martin Buber, *On the Bible*

I

. . . that morning as I stood at the window of the Capitol
and looked down on the crowd, I felt like God, because
I had the knowledge of what was to come. I felt like
God brooding on History, for as I stood there I could see
a little chunk of History right there in front. There were
the bronze statues on their pedestals, on the lawn, in
frock coats, with the right hand inserted under the coat,
just over the heart, in military uniforms with a hand on
the sword hilt, even one in buckskin with the right hand
grasping the barrel of a grounded long rifle. They were
already History, and the grass around their pedestals was
shaved close and the flowers were planted in stars and
circles and crescents. Then over beyond the statues, there
were the people who weren't History yet. Not quite. But
to me they looked like History, because I knew the end
of the event of which they were part. Or thought I knew
the end.

The soliloquist brooding on History is Jack Burden, narrator and inside man of Robert Penn Warren's *All the
King's Men.* This passage occurs toward the end of Chapter

1

III, when Burden awaits the outcome of impeachment proceedings against Willie Stark. Looking out the window, he assumes the stance and rhetoric of the prophet; he acts as a privileged witness with knowledge of what must come, but helpless to prevent catastrophe. Burden knows "the end of the event" because he has helped to pressure Stark's political enemies; he has himself played an equivocal, even corrupt part in the historical drama. His name, suggesting a humour character, testifies to the burdens he carries: the multiple role of actor and prophet, research historian and Ancient Mariner.

One word, *History*, dominates Burden's meditation. The word resonates with implication; Warren means us to hear vast metaphysical music as he repeats the word again and again. Capitalization, to reenforce textual eminence, reminds us of Carlyle who, in good German fashion, capitalized his nouns, especially those signifying The Terrible Abstractions. But Warren's capitals indicate nervous irony as he faces great intellectual problems; he writes with the self-consciousness of modern writers when they try out ideas: "I am tough and cool; I distrust philosophical and theological terminology; yet, when the chips are down, I too, like Tolstoy and Dostoevsky, can speculate on Knowledge, the End of Man, and The Enigma of History."

Two separate meanings of *History* emerge from our quoted passage. Both concern knowledge. Classically understood, history was what the human race remembered of its significant past; the historian's purpose was, in the words of Herodotus, to immortalize "the great and wonderful deeds of Greeks and barbarians." History was exemplary knowledge, preserving for future generations what might otherwise sink into oblivion. The passage remembers the classical concept; Burden tells us "he could see a little chunk of History right there in front. There were the bronze statues on their pedestals. . . . They were already History. . . ." However, Burden goes beyond remembering. He ventures to predict *who* will be immortalized in History: ". . . there were the people who weren't History yet. Not quite. But to me they looked like History, because I knew the end of the event of which they were a part. . . ." *History* also denotes knowledge of what will come to be.

Burden is filled with a sense of mantic power. Since the gods do not invest men with prophetic eloquence for trivial purposes, Burden names as *History* events he both witnesses and foretells. But we hear ironic undertones. The repetitions and quasi-theological capitalizations develop the familiar rhetorical excesses of the kitsch ideology that dignifies all happenings as History. The prophets of the media talk about "history-making events" which will take place next week; pop-revolutionaries reassure each other that History is on the side of the latest ideological fad. In our history-blighted epoch the common man and the uncommon man make History. No one is excluded from immortality: we no longer have Heaven but we do have History.

History denotes knowledge of past and future; it also circumscribes a wider range of concepts. At the center is the idea of process, the belief that history comprehends an order of antecedent cause and consequent effect; that this order moves purposively toward some goal; that this goal might also constitute an end to history—in theological language, an *eschaton*. Burden wrestles with the idea of historical process:

> For Life is a fire burning along a piece of string—or is it a fuse to a powder keg which we call God?—and the string is what we don't know, our Ignorance, and the trail of ash, which if a gust of wind does not come, keeps the structure of the string, is History, man's Knowledge, but it is dead, and when the fire has burned up all the string, then man's Knowledge will be equal to God's Knowledge and there won't be any fire, which is Life. Or if the string leads to a powder keg, then there will be a terrific blast of fire, and even the trail of ash will be blown completely away.

The passage is hardly clear; the eye of the mind is dazzled by the metaphorical fireworks. The syntax, on a long string of copulatives, struggles toward an articulation which equates Life, Ignorance, History, Knowledge, and God. Life burns along the string which then becomes either the ash of Knowledge or the shape of Ignorance. History, which is dead Knowledge, is determined by "the structure of the string." It all may lead to God (no certainty here); but God is the powder keg, the apocalypse and the end of History. As we sift out the meanings, one dominates: that historical process is violent. Man's life moves toward disaster. God, the biblical Lord of History, is Himself imaged in violent metaphor. And He is no longer distinct from the energies behind historical process. Sinister implications emerge as He becomes the mysterious agent generating events. Cass Mastern, Jack Burden's *alter ego* and the tragic subject of his abandoned doctoral dissertation, sees the God-Who-Is-History in a dreadful image of instinctual animality:

> [Cass Mastern] learned that the world is like an enormous spider web and if you touch it, however lightly, at any point, the vibration ripples to the remotest perimeter and the drowsy spider feels the tingle and is drowsy no more but springs out to fling the gossamer coils about you who have touched the web and then inject the black, numbing poison under your hide. It does not matter whether or not you meant to brush the web of things . . . what happens always happens and there is the spider, bearded black and with his great faceted eyes glittering like mirrors in the sun, or like God's eye, and the fangs dripping.

Warren, in this passage, does not specifically call the agent lurking behind catastrophe *History;* however, he leaves no doubt that Cass Mastern's foot on the web of the world stimulates historical process. Warren suggests, in similar tropes, that the process needs no stimulation. History may act with animal swiftness whether we disturb the universe or not. Merely to come within History's orbit of attack is sufficient to become a victim of the process. (The following brief poem is from Warren's *You, Emperors, and Others*):

> CRICKET, ON KITCHEN FLOOR, ENTERS HISTORY
> *History, shaped like white hen,*
> *Walked in at kitchen door.*
> *Beak clicked once on stone floor.*
> *Out door walked hen then;*
> *But will no doubt, come again.*

Historical process is aggressively evil in the image of the spider-God; it is merely fortuitous in the innocent activity of the chicken. The process, in both cases, is dynamic, destructive, and eschatological. History hungers; History strikes with animal swiftness and accuracy; History brings its victims to final things. In Warren's scheme it would seem that *History*, in the sense of process, replaces older notions of fate, but there is no contextual consistency. Warren plays a set of semantic variations on the word, first implying one meaning, then adumbrating another. At the conclusion of *All the King's Men*, Warren drops his insistent capitalization and ceases to view historical process as a metaphysical monster. He explains the *meaning of history* when he urges his peroration: ". . . soon now we shall go out of history and into history and the awful responsibility of time." The theory of history here is Old Testament-Prophetic: where history is conceived as a great moral drama and its meaning is never now but always to come; where the individual does not have complete control over his destiny but nevertheless must bear his burden of guilt and pay the penalty for every action. Before Warren reaches this conclusion he explores what *History* means, both as knowledge and process, in all its labyrinthine implications.

Warren's speculations oscillate between two large clusters of related concepts. History is knowledge: knowledge of what happened, of what is happening, of what might happen tomorrow. History is process: an immortal dialectic of opposing forces; a steady progression toward disaster; or, a great cycle, like the eternal return of the seasons, uniting beginning and end. Questions of moral discrimination tend to disappear. History is no longer the memory of worthy deeds; it is the memory of everything. All remembering is called history; all knowledge is subsumed, willy-nilly, under historical knowledge. As the epistemic authority of history widens, as every kind of social and political process is felt to be historical process, we discover that history achieves unique ontological status and becomes more than the means for uncovering reality. History names reality itself. Man cannot ignore historical knowledge, deadly though it may be, because it provides the ground of his being. Man cannot escape historical process because the process and his existence are identities. Existence is dynamic. What has come to be is the result of what has been; what will be, presumably, flows out of what is.

Warren's understanding of history as both knowledge and process, his identification of the process with the powder keg, the spider, and the chicken—with images of irrational violence—his insistent repetitions of *History* which develop a momentum of implication so powerful that the word, even in neutral contexts, generates a current of feeling: all such instances penetrate an echoing landscape of shared assumptions. Our minds respond with prior knowledge, with what we subliminally hold about the process that relegates nations to the trash heap and the knowledge that incapacitates men for action. Our minds, as receptacles for "beliefs which are so much a matter of course that they are rather tacitly presupposed than formally expressed,"[1] visualize History more as an avenging than a recording angel. History is a form of energy as well as the recollection of the past; history is life in an age of permanent crisis. Clio, that delicate muse, has been strangely metamorphosed and multiplied; history has been transformed from a category of human understanding to the substance and flux of life itself. In our life and in our literature, history has become radical reality.

2

The presuppositions about the nature and meaning of history originate in modern historicism and in the various dialectical movements issuing from it. Unfortunately, historicism as an intellectual movement is variously interpreted; historians, social and political philosophers, and literary critics hold contradictory and combative views.[2] Simply as a word, as a term describing a variety of phenomena, historicism is used both dyslogistically and honorifically. "Historicism" describes (and frequently disparages) methods of sociological analysis and literary scholarship; it honors our cultural heritage; it analyzes a state of mind, ascendant throughout the nineteenth century but now on the wane; or it discovers, gleaming through mists of metaphysics, the *Weltanschauung* itself. Undercutting all discussion of historicism is this paradox: that both polemics directed against historicism and eulogies advanced in its favor express themselves in historicist terms.

My understanding of historicism is neither methodological nor polemical; historicism is inescapable fact. Modern categories of knowing and understanding are historical; historical preconceptions are the Kantian "green glasses" with which we view the phenomenal world. The intense awareness that contemporary people share of living in a modern world and that this world developed out of a series of antecedent causes is basic to historicism. We know we are moderns and we say so. We are immersed in reality, in existence; but the nature of existence, how it came to be the way it is, is conceived as dynamic and historical.

Historicism entered modern intellectual life with the romantic movement. Hegel's *Philosophy of History* raised belief in the reality of historical process to a metaphysical imperative; it initiated not only speculation about the nature and dominant ontological status of history but also, in a way Hegel never intended, set in motion political forces that changed the world. Opposition to historicism, developed most dramatically in Nietzsche's work, is characterized by a profound (and often destructive) skepticism concerning the value of historical knowledge and a yearning for an end to history: for the Apocalypse. Hegel sits as Messiah, at the right hand of the God-Who-Is-History. Nietzsche walks the earth as Antichrist, antagonist of all who historicize reality and make history the ground of moral judgment. He diagnosed "the consuming fever of history" as a symptom of his century's sickness and prescribed drastic therapy for its devotion to the past. He prophesied how this devotion might weaken human personality, affect political development, and mold the substance of literary work.

We consider and compare Hegel's *Philosophy of History* and Nietzsche's *Untimely Meditation,* "Of the Use and Disadvantage of History for Life." Such a comparison offers a critical approach to historicism and a point of departure. "Of the Use and Disadvantage of History for Life" begins with an attack on the "historical culture" so assiduously promoted in nineteenth-century Germany. Nietzsche's contemporaries pointed to this culture with self-satisfied pride and regarded it as unique evidence of their moral superiority. Nietzsche acidly comments, ". . . a hypertrophic virtue—such as the modern 'historical sense'—can bring a nation to ruin as surely as a hypertrophic vice."[3] Too much history renders

modern man (especially if he is German) proud, oversophisti-
cated, and decadent. He becomes bored through knowing too
much and knowing how it all happened. And the present
loses its savor and immediacy; it is merely part of the panorama
ceaselessly rolling before jaded eyes. By the time Nietzsche
wrote his *Meditation,* belief in the Hegelian World-Process had
already suffered its dialectical transformation; a mysterious but
provocative notion (part of the nihilism Nietzsche feared) of
historical decline had replaced Hegel's belief in steady
progress. Man becomes an epigone; he believes in the old age
of the world and in himself as a late survivor, an impotent
witness to the power of History:

> *Shape without form, shade without color,*
> *Paralyzed force, gesture without motion . . .*

An accumulation of historical knowledge makes it impossible for man to forget; unless he can put the past behind him,
he cannot act creatively. History diminishes human energy
and the capacity for action. Too much history also begets too
much criticism. "The weakness of modern personality betrays
itself in the extravagance of critical gush, in the lack of
mastery over the self, in what the Romans called *impotentia.*"[4]
Art turns to parody and critique; artists despair of originality
and see present life as an ironical existence overshadowed by
the past: "Historical culture is, in reality, a form of congenital
grayheadedness; and those bearing its mark must come to
believe instinctively in the old age of mankind."[5]

Nietzsche attacks the pieties and superstitions attached to
the value of historical knowledge. But history is more than the
paralyzing hand of the past; Nietzsche carries the battle to
the metaphysical level. He repudiates the "disguised theology"
issuing from Hegel's *Philosophy of History;* he denounces
Hegel's attempt to explain the totality of history and denies
the existence of a World-Process and The Self-Realizing Idea:

> Truly disabling and discordant is the belief that one is
> a late-comer of the age: but it must seem frightful and
> shattering when one day, by an impudent reversal, such
> a belief apotheosizes this late-comer as the true goal and
> meaning of everything that previously transpired; when

his conscious suffering is set up as the perfection of
world-history. Such a point of view has made it habitual
for Germans to talk of "The World-Process," and to justify
their own time as the inevitable result of this World
Process; such a point of view has put history in the
place of the spiritual forces, art and religion, as sole
sovereign—to the extent that it is "The Dialectic of the
National Spirit," and "The Tribunal of the World."[6]

Hegel located the World-Spirit within time and history;
all events and actions expressed the Spirit—more exactly, embodied the Spirit. History presented a spectacle of ceaseless
change; Hegel was fully conscious that he lived in a dissolving
world. But the world dissolved and changed in order to renew itself. Although *The Philosophy of History* teems with
passages evoking the pathos of universal mutability, Hegel saw
change as essentially positive: "death is the issue of life, life is
also the issue of death." *The Philosophy of History* is informed
by a passionate optimism:

> The general thought—the category which first presents
> itself in this restless mutation of individuals and peoples,
> existing for a time and then vanishing—is that of *change*
> at large. The sight of the ruins of some ancient sovereignty
> directly leads us to contemplate this thought of change
> in its negative aspect. What traveler among the ruins of
> Carthage, of Palmyra, Persepolis, or Rome, has not been
> stimulated to reflections on the transiency of kingdoms
> and men, and to sadness at the thought of a vigorous
> and rich life now departed. . . . But the next consideration
> which allies itself with that of change, is, that change while
> it imports dissolution, involves at the same time the rise
> of a *new life*—that while death is the issue of life, life
> is also the issue of death. This is a grand conception; one
> which the Oriental thinkers attained, and which is per-
> haps the highest in their metaphysics. In the idea of
> *Metempsychosis* we find it evolved in its relation to indi-
> vidual existence; but a myth more generally known is
> that of the *Phoenix* as a type of the Life of *Nature;*
> eternally preparing for itself its funeral pyre, and con-
> suming itself upon it; but so that from its ashes is pro-
> duced the new, renovated, fresh life. But this image is

only Asiatic; oriental not occidental. Spirit—consuming
the envelope of its existence—does not merely pass into
another envelope, nor rise rejuvenescent from the ashes
of its previous form; it comes forth exalted, glorified, a
purer spirit. It certainly makes war upon itself—consumes its own existence; but in this very destruction it
works up that existence into a new form, and each successive phase becomes in turn a material, working on
which it exalts itself to a new grade.[7]

We note Hegel's passion for antinomies and their reconciliation. The Dialectic operates spiritually and materially, creatively and destructively, within events and upon events. It is
abstract thought and it is action; it is the dancer and the
dance, the dreamer and his dream. History agitates as internal principle, the activity of pure thought; it also realizes
itself in external existence. Spirit and being interrelate and
penetrate each other. A nation and its "national psychology,"
the so-called "spirit of a people,"

. . . erects itself into an objective world, that exists and
persists in a particular form of religious worship, customs, constitution, and political laws—in the whole complex of institutions—in the events and transactions that
make up its history. That is its work—that is what this
particular Nation *is*. Nations are what their deeds are.[8]

Immersed in change, Hegel historicizes reality; eternity
does not lie outside of time but remains forever within, in-
tegral to the process. The Dialectic is presumably immortal,
and historical process goes on forever. It is precisely in change
that permanence resides. Christian philosophers of history saw
God as the unmoved mover, "At the still point of the turning
world"; history and its pattern of continual change revealed
God to the world. God could never change because He resided
outside time. But Hegel moved a significant step further and
concludes (as Ernst Cassirer puts it) that "history is no mere
appearance of God, but his reality: God not only 'has' history,
he *is* history."[9]

Nietzsche wished men to live beyond history and the world
of transitory things. He believed, like Hegel, in the dialectical

nature of existence; the world was struggle and process. But he saw no redemption in ceaseless change and turmoil. Nietzsche's reading of Hegel made man not the hero of the historical process but its victim. History could not justify God's ways to men; Hegel's naming his method a theodicy was particularly troublesome. Such method encouraged the belief that raw power is the final arbiter in human affairs. (Nietzsche foretold the political effects of Hegelian doctrine as he foretold the misuses to which his own philosophy would be put.) Power cannot be impugned without impugning the "rightness" of historical proces—and the process, "this Idea or Reason . . . the True, the Eternal, the Absolute Power" is God. Within Hegel's framework any action may become morally justifiable simply because it happened; or more arrogantly, because it might happen. Trotsky's sweeping Martov "into the ashcan of History," or Khrushchev's threatening, "We shall bury you, History is on our side," are more than ill-bred displays of party-line rhetoric; they are blasphemous appeals to Hegel's God-Who-Is-History. As Nietzsche feared, Hegel's philosophy of history became the favored doctrine of the successful: "[Hegel] has planted in generations, thoroughly leavened by him, that worship before 'The Power of History' which suddenly converts every moment into naked admiration of success and leads to idolatry of the actual."

Hegel entered the nineteenth century confident that man could redeem himself in historical existence; the Spirit, refined and refining, would cast out all that was irrelevant, contradictory, or circumstantial. Nietzsche entered the twentieth century prophesying "wars the like of which has never existed on earth," the end of historical existence. Hegel saw God alive in history, man's existence in his acts, and the dialectical process reconciling the two. Nietzsche mourned the death of God, saw man's will emasculated by historical knowledge, and urged, in desperation, a redemptive leap to eternity. Nietzsche saw no salvation in history; quite the contrary: "All history is the refutation by experiment of the notion of the so-called 'moral world order.' "[10] With the death of God, twenty centuries of Christian world-history reached disorderly conclusion.

Nietzsche's denial of Hegelian historical process left a void. He could not believe that the world was without purpose; this would mean embracing the nihilism he so feared. The philosophic examination of existence must yield an Ariadne-thread through the labyrinth of suffering and joy. Nietzsche advanced in *Zarathustra* the myth of Eternal Recurrence: not as a philosophy of history but a philosophy *against* history. Hegel noted that the Spirit was no phoenix, reliving the same life again and again; the Spirit "elaborates on existence," rising higher and higher in its successive transformations. Hegel looked backward on ruin, forward toward progress; in Hegel's system the present moment scarcely existed. But for Nietzsche every moment was a pregnant psychological fact; he prized the moment and denied that human events showed moral teleology. The pattern of the past and metaphysical systems were mind-forged manacles. The myth of Eternal Recurrence affirmed the moment and the individual against historical change and the deadly power that cried against Zarathustra: "All things pass away; therefore all things deserve to pass away."[11] The forms of human experience do not vary; psychologically understood, the same things happen again and again. Man, like Blake's Mental Traveler, eternally suffers the traumas of birth and death, the torments of pain and ecstasy. Man's reconciliation to this doom, a joyous *amor fati*, is the measure of his salvation. Nietzsche reverses the Hegelian formula that man's nature is determined by his history—his significant history issues from his nature, from what he possesses of intellectual character and powerful feelings.

Nietzsche owed much to Hegelian method; Eternal Recurrence and the Dialectic proceed by contradiction, by the swirling opposition of polarities. But if Hegel was content to accept the judgments of history, Nietzsche urged a transcendent repudiation of faith in a redemptive historical process. Zarathustra yearns for eternity, *tiefe, tiefe, Ewigkeit;* and gnashes his teeth when he remembers the past:

> But now learn this as well: the will itself is still a prisoner. Willing liberates: but what do we name that which also throws the liberator into chains? "It was"—

that is the name of the will's gnashing of teeth and loneliest affliction. Powerless against what has been done, he is an angry witness of all that is past.[12]

Life, Nietzsche never tires of saying, must dominate knowledge; men must learn to think and act unhistorically: without self-consciousness and that embarrassed sense of irony cultivated in modern museum culture. The Higher Criticism of the nineteenth century demythologized, through history, religious belief; Nietzsche wished to dehistoricize, through his mythologies of *der Übermensch* and Eternal Recurrence, prevailing concerns of knowledge and value. He set himself deliberately against his age; his purpose and being, he proclaimed, were to be untimely, against the pressure of the past and the distorting power of change. Nietzsche had the radical intuition which permitted him to see the tendencies of the nineteenth century hardening into the dilemmas of the twentieth. That Nietzsche found no redemption from time and history save in his own madness; that the scum of the earth, in his name, made death, not life, triumph over knowledge and came close to destroying historical culture, are terrible ironies and occasions for pity and despair.

3

We have noted that the myth of Eternal Recurrence was not a philosophy *of* history but "a philosophy *against* history." Nietzsche had no interest in interpreting the particularities of events; he was interested in what men must do to live in meaningful contact with existence. And like all myth, the Eternal Recurrence explains action and existence in profoundly paradoxical, even contradictory terms. Nietzsche first presents the concept of recurrence in *The Gay Science;* an allegorical demon whispers into mankind's ear:

"This life, as you now live it, and have lived it, you must live again and again, times without number; and there will be nothing new in it, but every pain and every joy and every thought and sigh and everything unspeakably small or great in your life must return again to you: and all in the same order and sequence . . . The eternal hour-glass of existence is turned over again and again—and you with it, a speck of dust."[13]

Nietzsche elaborates the concept of recurrence as a direct challenge to the linear, Christian theology of history. To discover that life, in all its forms, is eternally reborn becomes a tremendous source of hope. Another Nietzschean demon (in *Zarathustra*) mutters, "All that is straight lies. . . . All truth is crooked; time itself is a circle." No myth can be complete without a god; and Nietzsche elevated Dionysus, his dialectical contender against Christ, to be the active symbol of Eternal Recurrence: "The God on the cross is a curse on life, a pointer to seek redemption from it; Dionysus cut to pieces is a *promise* of life: it is eternally reborn and comes back from destruction."[14]

Nietzsche's use of myth points forward to twentieth-century rediscovery of mythical thought to order the "facts" of history. Spengler and Toynbee buttress their historical findings with a mythical framework; Yeats in *A Vision* and the poetry derived from it, Eliot in *The Waste Land,* and Thomas Mann in much of his major work, use myth to parody, to parallel, or to intensify human experience. This study deals with the idea of history as it reveals itself in modern literature; it deals essentially with the burdens imposed by historical knowledge and the supposed structure of events, the historical process. The question now arises: does the study concern itself with history in Ranke's celebrated sense, *wie es eigentlich gewesen* (in the current argot of The People, "like it really was, man!"), or does it uncover a varied mythology?

A story told about Hegel and *The Philosophy of History* may offer some instruction. A student complained to the master that "the facts of history" could not be comfortably fitted into Hegel's metaphysical scheme. "So much the worse for 'the facts,' " was Hegel's magisterial reply. Any theory or philosophy of history only very imperfecty fits all the facts; any elaborate philosophy of history, such as Spengler's or Toynbee's, distorts, either through omission or selective inclusion, the "facts" of history. All highly schematic theories of history approach myth; Spengler's vision of cultural dissolution and Yeats's vision of the gyres are both mythical readings of history. Philip Wheelwright points out, in a brilliantly suggestive passage, that the Hegelian Dialectic itself may have its origins in primitive modes of thought. The triadic form of the Dialectic closely resembles mythic patterns found in Greek and eastern religious belief.[15]

The current critical conflict between "history" and "myth" is largely a rhetorical encounter. The History invoked by Marxist and neo-Marxist critics as superior to or more "real" than the myths which inhabit modern works of the imagination is itself a mythical creation. Philip Rahv complains that the concern with myth originates in ". . . the fear of history. It is feared because modern life is above all an historical life producing changes with vertiginous speed. . . ." Rahv then allegorizes History as the Powerhouse which grinds up the past ". . . as so much raw material in the fabrication of an unthinkable future."[16] Rahv, in his polemical zeal, creates his own myth of History in recognizable Marxist form: History is a dispenser of justice and the determining power in an age of necessity and fate. It is not difficult to see that the Hegelian-Marxist History is, in its lineaments and proportions, as pure a myth as Nietzschean recurrence or Augustine's City of God.

I would not like to appear to be playing a semantic shell game with the counters "history" and "myth." However, it is clear that theories interpreting historical process take mythical shapes when they enter literary imagination. This is true of works of rarefied literary sophistication; it is also true of works of purported historicity. Joyce's *Finnegans Wake* turns on a "commodius vicus of recirculation," Vico's version of the myth of historical recurrence. Trotsky's *History of the Russian Revolution* apotheosizes History as an avenging god, an almost Aeschylean personification of Force and an agency of human redemption. Joyce's Viconian myth of recurrence and Trotsky's Marxist myth of History represent reifications of the two basic ideas in which Western thought has conceptualized the historical process. The manifold versions of historical recurrence are based on a cyclical idea which views the processes of history as analogous to, or identical with, natural processes and ultimately to the cycle of the tides and seasons, and the

alternation of day and night. Marx's vision of History derives
from Hegel's secularization of the Jewish-Christian idea of
history. The prophets of the Old Testament saw history as a
linear movement toward the advent of the Messiah and toward
redemption in the Promised Land. The Christian modification
of the Old-Testament idea promises salvation not in the
earthly city of Jerusalem but in the City of God. A line to
salvation pierces human existence to reach beyond existence
and touch God's obscure but just Purpose. Thus both the
Jewish and Christian ideas of history posit an *eschaton,* a final
event which supposedly brings history to its appointed end.
Marx's *eschaton* is the classless society; the state has "withered
away" and men live redeemed from those misfortunes suffered
in historical existence.

Certainly the most dramatic feature of both the Jewish-
Christian and Marxist visions of history is what Frank Kermode calls "eschatological threat": the persistent anxiety that
God or the Dialectic will violently suspend historical process.[17]
The poets and novelists of this study might be labeled con-
noisseurs of apocalypse. They anticipate an end which will
come in an epic struggle between Christ and Antichrist or between the proletariat and the bourgeoisie. Some writers embrace the idea of the end with an extravagant *amor fati*—such
an idea lends symbolic resonance and dramatic depth to
literary work. Others react with fear and trembling. From the
dry month of *Gerontion* and *The Waste Land* to the pente-
costal fire of "Little Gidding," Eliot speaks of last things.
Malraux's novels about the revolutionary struggle of the Left
resound with the fury of *la lutte finale*. Mann's *Doctor Faustus*
takes us *through* the German apocalypse to a point somewhere
beyond the end—where we can faintly hear a single note of
hope.

Whether our century has witnessed an apocalypse, whether
we have relived in our politics the last days of the Roman
Empire, are hardly matters subject to precise historical verification. Literary myth is not open to scientific confirmation; it
becomes a metaphoric structure open to interpretation. Apocalypse, Kermode notes, is always happily "disconfirmed"; the
time for the end comes and goes—and the world somehow
manages to survive. But the myth of apocalypse is hardly

"irrelevant." The world of action and the world of literature are not sealed off from each other; the myths of recurrence and redemptive world-history have had the profoundest implications. These speculations raise myriad problems of value and this study moves between literary and political criticism. However, I try to measure the political significance of a writer not by the number of assertions he makes on current issues and partisan matters but by the success with which he brings his readers into imaginative contact with what Yeats calls "the desolation of reality." We learn, then, that *The Waste Land* has more to say than Marx on the problem of alienation; that "The Second Coming" gives a more shocking evaluation of totalitarianism than the polemics of the New Left. Each writer in this study apprehends the way modern life *feels* as it moves through historical existence; he makes moral assumptions based on an ideal relationship between man and the community in which he lives. Such apprehension and such assumptions are, in the higher ideology generated by successful creative work, profoundly political.

This ideology is neither reactionary nor conservative, but in the literal sense of that overused term, *radical*. Fear of the gathering momentum of historical process and skepticism toward the value of historical knowledge informed a literature which abrogated nineteenth-century liberalism. Feeling themselves victims of history, modern writers have not affirmed the cardinal principles of liberal doctrine: man's inherent goodness and the uninterrupted forward movement of historical process. Because history (as knowledge) told so much about the past of the race, the origins of religion, and (through Freud) the genesis of mind, writers grew ambiguous toward knowledge and uncertain about culture. Because history (as process) gave birth to a new century marked by war and revolution, writers grew alienated from the progressive myths of their fathers and collapsed into anxieties about apocalypse. Those who struggled with Gustav von Aschenbach between Apollo and Dionysus, those who inhabited the cactus country of spiritual deprivation, those who saw the Rough Beast issue from *Anima Mundi*, could hardly adapt themselves to the flabby rigors of positive thinking.

The First World War convinced a generation of poets

and novelists that history was a malign destiny. The essential
modernity of the literature which flourished between World
Wars is epitomized in these questions. What is the fate of
western civilization? Where has the historical process situated
Europe in the twentieth century? How has the process destroyed or negated the inherited past? To what extent has
knowledge of the past contributed to the bleakness of the
present moment? A myth about the nature of historical process
and the value of historical knowledge resides in each of these
questions. This study is indeed concerned with mythical thinking and its rendering of attitudes toward our subject. The
method and vocabulary of myth have increasingly shaped
literary attitudes toward history—not because serious writers
thought they could escape the exactions of living in an age of
desperate crisis but because history offered war and revolution,
the destruction of inherited values, and a shocking decay in the
quality of life. As the classical concept of history lost its
validity and power, as traditional belief in the value of
knowledge was eroded, and as writers grew skeptical about
the future, the Muse of Memory evolved into that ominous
metaphysical monster: History.

4

I do not propose a New Historical Criticism which explains
how the *was*-ness of the past enters an existentially conceived
is-ness of the present. Nor do I systematically separate out
philosophy of history as it appears in literary work—although
philosophical thought, metaphorically and mythically transformed, informs modern writing. Rather, I explore the double
meaning of *history* and the various ways this meaning functions as an internal principle within literary work. *History*
emerges as concrete and discrete meaning. An attitude toward
history may be revealed in technical procedures: programmatic
anachronism, fluctuating metric, and fragmented syntax reflect, in *The Waste Land,* Eliot's preoccupation with past and
present. Yeats's prophetic poems and *A Vision* are based on a
highly schematized mythology which "explains," albeit in a
thoroughly unhistorical way, the putative working of historical
process. Thomas Mann's *The Magic Mountain,* a work assess-

ing the health of European culture from a shifting perspective of contrary values, operates within a context of historical assumptions.

The link binding together the work of writers in this study is the strenuous knowledge of having lived in history as functioning organs of the world's body. Their knowledge is not preconceived; what they know is discovered, the knowledge of their own blood and nerves. It comes more from insight than theory. These writers are, in Ezra Pound's phrase, "antennae of the race"; the signals they receive are urgent bulletins on social stability and cultural health. They challenge, often with Nietzschean skepticism, the wisdom of old men. Is the past only a jumble of quotations, fragments to shore against ruin? Is historical process the matrix of rough beasts? Does the world end with a bang or a whimper? The questions are not didactic excursions or moral tags; they give form to the works they animate. They are rehearsed in the tormented dialectic on The Magic Mountain and in the weary pilgrimage to The City of God. They issue from the heightened historical consciousness—which is prophecy.

The writer-as-prophet is an equivocal figure. What he understands is rarely sought and seldom desired. His subject seeks him and he is, in a sense, its victim. The Idea (or Nightmare) of History sought out the writers of this study. Each reacted with characteristic rhetorical gestures; each assumed the deliberate disguise of his form. Adams is the ironic analyst of the life and career of a failure he calls *Henry Adams*. Eliot wonders whether he may not be mad or incited by "backward devils"—Dante's false prophets with their heads screwed toward the rear. Mann's prophetic rage is concealed behind the receptive naïveté of Hans Castorp or the coldly demonic impersonality of Adrian Leverkühn. But controlling the gestures of rhetoric, working behind the strategies of form, is the sensibility that has lived close to radical reality. It sees history asserting its transcendent will and revealing its obscure purpose. Such knowledge, often terrifying, earns our forgiveness. Without it we perish in ignorance; with it we may understand our destiny and defy augury.

II

Henry Adams

". . . he found himself lying in the Gallery of Machines
at the Great Exposition of 1900, his historical neck broken
by the sudden irruption of forces totally new."
—*The Education of Henry Adams*

I

Nietzsche was little more than a name to Henry Adams; we
have no record that Adams knew the meditation "Of the Use
and Disadvantage of History"—or that Adams ever read a line
of Nietzsche.[1] Yet doubtless he would have recognized himself,
with his usual ironic self-deprecation, as one of Nietzsche's
epigones: a latecomer into the world of Steam and Democracy,
congenitally gray-headed and ill-equipped to endure frantic
years of being a "helpless victim," waiting to be sent "he
knew not where."[2] In his calmer moments Adams tells us he
was a "consenting, contracting party"[3] to his life and career;
but more often the voice of *The Education* and his letters
assumes the inflections of a blackly humorous observer and
suffering target of historical forces.

It is this persona, hugely present, that shall be the Henry
Adams of my consideration. He appears as witness and victim,
as malign critic of his age, and, of course, as prophet. This
persona is projected large over recent literary discussion,
and Adams emerges as something of a culture-hero. As a culture-hero I intend to regard him. I make no attempt to fathom
the other Adams who lurks behind the irritable temper and
bitter self-mockery of the letters and the mannered diffidence

and outrageously coy understatements of *The Education.* Adams endured terrible suffering and often gave terrible expression to his suffering; he sustained the disappointments of his personal life with admirable stoicism—but he also gave the age in which he lived holy and particular hell.

One tack is to regard Adams as an American Nietzsche. Such comparison is voluntaristic and rhetorical; Adams had neither Nietzsche's powerful gift of psychological insight nor his poetic imagination. Nor did Adams have the explosive effect Nietzsche had; he did not influence an entire generation and help bring his prophecies to fulfillment. But Adams's personal development, his temperament and style, his current relevance, all touch on Nietzsche's life and work. They both served academic tenures. Both did brilliant work in the historical disciplines and both declared, with passionate vehemence, that they were spoiled by an excess of historical knowledge. Both became polemicists against their age. Adams precariously controlled vast currents of interior violence; like Nietzsche, he frequently vented his despair and frustration in extreme statements. From extremity Nietzsche passed into insanity and finally silence. Adams's later years were disfigured by a hysterical advocacy of violence and pathological anti-Semitism. Both hated their century and the supposed cultural squalor, the aesthetic deprivation of democratic existence. Both predicted (and hoped) that the civilization they so hated would be destroyed in some unnamable cataclysm. Both perfected a literary style of epigrammatic brilliance; reading their books is a journey into mined territory. We are blown up by astonishing insights and prophecies which long ago turned out true.

A temperamental similarity shows in their aggressive literary style—the style of those whom Edwin Muir calls "pseudo men-of-action."[4] Pseudo men-of-action—Carlyle, Nietzsche, Spengler, and Adams—never leave the study but with hot polemical zeal cheer loudly the brutal behavior of others. They live in a dream of action and history. In his unbuttoned moments Adams displays a ferocious taste for vicarious violence. His letters to Elizabeth Cameron on the Dreyfus Affair reveal him a two-fisted partisan of the anti-Dreyfusards and a delighted spectator of the Paris riots: "But Zola howled; and the

Bourse actually fought—Jews against Gentiles—till the police came in. A good day's work! and rioting too in Havana! and a new outbreak in India! *Tiens! ça marche!* One can't imagine larks like this every day, to be sure . . ."[5]

I am aware of Adams's heavy-handed ambivalence. He knows and does not know it is cruel to enjoy violence; he cannot resist taking a small boy's pleasure in observing the world proceed to blow itself up. He cannot resist (to cite Yvor Winters) the temptation "to be witty rather than intelligent."[6] On such matters as "the antisemitic ravings of Drumont"[7] or the innocence of "the howling Jew Dreyfus"[8] Adams prefers irony to understanding, wisecracks to humanity. Adams became a victim of his own irony—that aggressive defense against the misfortunes of his life and the alarming developments in his country, in the world of burgeoning scientific development, and in international affairs. He would not avert his gaze; he was repelled by the excesses he noted and analyzed, fascinated by the enormities he predicted. Irony allowed him to come to terms with the raging disorders of the outer world and the inner world of his own personality—which, in its perverse way, yearned for the chaos it abhorred.

Like Nietzsche, Adams became a critic and moralist of knowledge. He was a trained and skillful historian and spent long years working at his profession. His instinct and passion for order led him back to medieval Europe which he envisioned as a single culture with the Blessed Virgin as presiding female deity. This vision of a homogeneous Middle Ages is celebrated in his most serene attempt at historical reconstruction, *Mont-Saint-Michel and Chartres*. Adams does not seek the "truth" about the Middle Ages; indeed, he admits "The twelfth and thirteenth centuries, studied in the pure light of political economy, are insane." Rather, he sees the thirteenth century through the great rose window at Chartres and in the light streaming from the Virgin. The unity he discovers exists in carefully selected details, in the delightful fiction that the sexual energy emanating from Our Lady brought ultimate meaning into the chaos of medieval life.

Mont-Saint-Michel and Chartres is a beautiful and touching effort to see pattern in the life of the past. But in the shadowed world of the later nineteenth century, Adams painfully discovers that historical knowledge is without pattern or significance, that history is no longer knowledge but the brute violence of irrational energies. History is not the poetic evocation of architecture" . . . and the last and greatest deity of all, the Virgin. . . ." History is the Dynamo shocking modern men and their society into near insensibility; our guiding trope for this belief is given in Chapter XXV of *The Education:*

> Satisfied that the sequence of men led to nothing and that the sequence of their society could lead no further . . . while the mere sequence of thought was chaos, he turned at last to the sequence of force; and thus it happened that, after ten years' pursuit, he found himself lying in the Gallery of Machines at the Great Exposition of 1900, his historical neck broken by the sudden irruption of forces totally new.

Adams rejects even the possibility of historical knowledge, for "the mere sequence of thought was chaos. . . ." But Adams's world was experiencing vast and terrible changes; *something* must be behind the decadence of the French aristocracy, the skulduggery of bankers and politicians, the disastrous financial panics which threatened to undermine the capital holdings of the Adams family. History may be unfathomable; historical process, however, is real and terrifying. Adams no longer regarded history as the informed and informing memory of man; history became History, the Powerhouse of Change, and was now invested with metaphysical significance. Adams felt he must understand not men, not events, not ideas but the dynamics of an inscrutable process.

His final, bleak hope was to discover historical "laws" based on stop-press scientific information. The posthumously published *The Degradation of the Democratic Dogma* expounds, in crude and confused analogic terms, a supposed "scientific" theory of history. The theory founders on the rocks of stubborn monism; on Adams's inability or unwillingness to differentiate between history and nature—between the world of matter and the world of men and ideas; and on Adams's desperate need for certainty and immediate answers to complex problems. Adams urges the discovery of "historical law":

> You may be sure that four out of five serious students of history who are living today have, in the course of their work, felt that they stood on the brink of a great generalization that would reduce all history under a law as clear as the laws which govern the material world . . . The law was certainly there, and as certainly was in places actually visible, to be touched and handled, as though it were a law of chemistry or physics. No teacher with a spark of imagination or with an idea of scientific method can have helped dreaming of the immortality that would be achieved by the man who should successfully apply Darwin's method to the facts of human history.[9]

Two long essays, "A Letter to American Teachers of History" and "The Rule of Phase Applied to History," elaborate the questionable thesis that history may be subsumed under natural science. The essays display dilettante scientism and incredible analogic gymnastics; one quotation may serve to illustrate Adams's method: ". . . the historical inquirer or experimenter . . . may assume, as his starting point, that Thought is a historical substance, analogous to an electric current, which obeyed the laws—whatever they are—of Phase. The hypothesis is not extravagant."[10] Adams wishes a predictive science of history; as the argument unwinds we discover The Rule of Phase—indeed all of Adams's theory of history—is not the formulation of scientific law but its radical opposite: thinly veiled prophetic utterance. "The law of phase," the law of inverse squares, the second law of thermodynamics—all of which figure in Adams's discourse—strike us as the familiar types and symbols of biblical prophecy:

> Signs are taken for wonders. "We would see a sign!"
> The word within a word, unable to speak a word,
> Swaddled in darkness.

An earlier essay, "The Tendency of History" (also included in The Degradation of the Democratic Dogma), is more restrained. Adams is ambivalent toward knowledge that portends a dismal future. He recognizes the self-fulfilling nature of prophecy and its peculiar ability to bring about exactly the catastrophes it warns against. Because his new "science of history" sees the certain downfall of traditional culture, Adams moves back from such knowledge. The world is not ready to hear about the triumph of communism and the overthrow of property. "Would society as now constituted tolerate the open assertion of a necessity which should affirm its approaching overthrow?"[11]

Adams hedges his belief in such a necessity. "The Tendency of History" was officially addressed to the American Historical Association and it sings the qualified music of academic caution. But in his letters and the posthumous *Education,* as a private party or a voice from the grave, Adams is hardly restrained about the decadence he everywhere sees. He reads Max Nordau's sensational *Entartung (Degeneration),* a journalistic product of the *fin de siècle,* and writes to Charles Milnes Gaskell, "The other day I thought I saw myself, but run mad and howling. I took up a book without noticing its title particularly and read a few pages. Then vertigo seized me, for I thought I must be inventing a book in a dream."[12] He encourages his brother Brooks to write *The Law of Civilization and Decay,* but carefully disassociates himself; he asks his "idiot brother"[13] to strike his name from the dedication page and declares, "I do not care to monkey with a dynamo."[14] Adams feels there is nothing to be gained in openly telling society what lies in wait.

Adams lived long enough to have the dubious satisfaction of knowing his insights and instincts were correct. The outbreak of the First World War came as a prophecy confirmed and he felt his theories were vindicated. Bernard Berenson, a frequent target for Adams's tirades, wrote him in 1914: "I trust that you are satisfied at last and that all your pessimistic hopes have been fulfilled."[15] Adams did not live to see the end of the war; symbolically enough, he died in the midst of the cataclysm he had so long predicted. Six months after his death came the publication of *The Education of Henry Adams.* With *The Education* Adams gradually emerged as a major figure among those intellectuals who sensed the direction of change and calculated its devastations.

Adams's restlessness, his neurotic scrupulosity, his frenzied
energy directed toward forcing answers from a silent cosmos
suggest that he succumbed to the irrationalism and anarchy
he so feared. He was deeply horrified at the break-up of the
old order; he consoled himself with the intensity of his
nihilistic utterances and "Tory anarchism." From one angle
of vision, his theory of history appears a job of massive rationalization, an undertaking to justify his unsuccess. Henry
Adams never lived in the White House, as did his grandfather
and great-grandfather; History and its mysterious energies
flowed against him. Adams's theory of history, with all its noise
and doom, appears vindictive and personal. We are tempted
to confute his theory in a polemical spirit: Adams, not getting
the world on his own terms, consigns it to Hell.

From another angle of vision, Adams's characterization of
historical energy is of crucial importance. The Dynamo and
Virgin make no contribution to the philosophy of history;
they provide metaphors for the literary imagination and
images of new, unfathomable forces in politics and society.
Symptomatic of an emerging mood, they suggest that human
behavior is based not on logical endeavor but on instinct and
unconscious and pre-conscious motivations. Adams takes his
place with Freud and Nietzsche, Bergson and Sorel, and the
other new men of the early twentieth century who were re-
discovering the irrational component of human thought and
action.

2

"The proper study of mankind is woman . . ."

Nietzsche's most celebrated parable dramatizes a madman cry-
ing out the death of God through the marketplace of the
modern world.[16] Opposed to the dead God is the living
Dionysus, Nietzsche himself, asserting a radical doctrine of
creativity against the life-destroyers of the nineteenth century.
The aging Henry Adams, "lying in the gallery of Machines
at the Great Exposition of 1900, his historical neck broken
by the sudden irruption of forces totally new," is an equally
dramatic image of the modern existential agony. Opposed to

the Dynamo and its pitiless rays of energy was the Virgin, Adams's beloved life symbol, *his* image of the creative principle. Adams's Virgin is no theological abstraction but wholly flesh and blood, maternal and sexual. Adams identifies Her with the divine patroness of Lucretius's *De Rerum Natura:*

> *Aeneadum genetrix, hominum divumque voluptas*
> *alma Venus . . .*

A wit summed up Santayana's ambivalent relationship to Roman Catholicism in this ironic credo: "There is no God and Mary is His Mother." Adams might have similarly expressed his idiosyncratic Mariolatry: "God has died and his Mother is my mistress."

Adams's fondness for the Virgin expresses a very high estimation of women and a personal susceptibility. He is most attractive in his excited and tender responsiveness to female sexuality. His letters from Samoa and Tahiti are suffused with an erotic awareness that edges close to pornography—if we adhere closely to standards current in Adams' day. Certainly the delight Adams shows in female nakedness is hardly expected from one who "brought up among the Puritans knew that sex was sin."

Adams came to think otherwise. He castigated American life for its prudish refusal to accept the joy and use the power of sexual experience; he recognized, long before D. H. Lawrence and Leslie Fiedler, the unhealthy sexlessness of classic American literature. American life was symptomatic; the problem was European, perhaps worldwide. Sexual vitality and creative energy were drying up at the wellsprings of civilization. And the desiccation of sexual life withered the religious impulse. Christianity died as the power of womanly influence diminished before masculine assault. "At times, the historian would have been almost willing to maintain that the man had overthrown the Church chiefly because it was feminine."[17] The Virgin, Alma Venus, no longer stood at the world's center; no lines of force emanated from modern woman. The loss of the female principle was a profound cultural deprivation and a grave spiritual sickness.

Adams saw civilization maintained at too severe a cost.

The modern world had technology and democracy, widening urbanization and increasing financial affluence. For these gifts of progress men paid an overwhelming psychic price. The competitive anxieties of industrial life subverted man's sexuality: "He could not run his machine and a woman too; he must leave her, even though his wife, to find her own way, and all the world saw her trying to find her way by imitating him."[18] A new race of women workers crowded factories and offices; the birth rate declined rapidly from Victorian plenitude. Adams saw that woman's identity suffered confusion; masculinity and femininity required new definitions and the act of love acquired meanings outside the sphere of children and family. He envisioned a sterile world of sexless men and unhappy, frustrated women. The men worshipped the Dynamo; Adams himself had offered blasphemous prayers: "Before the end, one began to pray to it; inherited instinct taught the natural expression of man before silent and infinite force."[19] Woman, isolated and driven, denied her sex by unmorally asserting it ("the American woman was oftener surprised at finding herself regarded as sexual");[20] by competing with men; or by entering the abyss of mental dislocation. Woman, severed from traditional stabilities, gained "equality" with her tormentor and quickly earned the privilege of sharing man's self-conscious anguish.

We need only to recall the impotent men and hysterical women of modern literature, avatars of the wounded Fisher King and abandoned Isolde, to find validation for Adams's anxieties. The Fisher King and Hyacinth Girl of *The Waste Land,* Clifford and Connie Chatterley, Jake Barnes and Lady Brett, Detlev Spinell and Gabriele Klöterjahn (of Thomas Mann's *Tristan*) are sexual cripples: sensitive, injured men who cannot make love; neurotic women, unsatisfied in both deprivation and excess. The loss of the female principle harrows Eliot's vision of urban despair, blackens the towns and landscapes of D. H. Lawrence's prophetic novels, and desolates the mountain refuges and Venetian seascapes of Hemingway and Mann. Failure in love is attributed to bourgeois brutality and insensitivity, to a mechanized, impersonal social order, and to the sickening catastrophe of world war. "That dirty war," the sympathetic *poule* remarks to Jake Barnes when he tells her he was hurt in the war. History frustrates the life-giving act of sex.

Virgin and Dynamo have often been remarked a grotesque antithesis. "The two symbols . . . ," Austin Warren tells us, "are not parallel."[21] The Dynamo is a mechanic fallacy, a perversely modern development of the romantic pathetic fallacy. Nature is no longer anthropomorphic, displaying human feeling and shedding human tears. Rather, nature and man become mechanized like those birds and beasts in animated cartoons who stop with a shrieking of brakes and fly with the noise of airplanes. Adams views history as he views the great machine of the universe noisily running down according to the second law of thermodynamics. But the trouble is not in the universe but in ourselves. Dynamo and Virgin are emblematic of human irrational energies; Adams finds History and Women equally unfathomable, impervious to understanding and incapable of explanation. The trouble resides underground, below conscious levels. Adams never brings to explicit formulation that the Dynamo and Virgin might represent the eternal polarities of destruction and creation, the human aggressive instinct and the human capacity for regeneration. Dynamo and Virgin resemble Freud's immortal antagonists, Thanatos and Eros. And Adams must have suspected, as Freud did toward the end of his life, that the "heavenly powers" of destruction and creation originate at the same dark center of the human soul.

3

Adams never suggests a reconciliation of Dynamo and Virgin. He mentions no possibility of a synthesis which might combine and recombine the antagonist forces. The energies are disparate, remote from each other in time and in mental space; they are equally remote as substances and causes. The Virgin was medieval, human, female, compassionate; the Dynamo is modern, mechanical, mindless, destructive. The Virgin was real substance; her work is that of Eros, "builder of cities." The Dynamo is that metaphysical monster, History; its work is annihilation. Between Dynamo and Virgin there can be no rapprochement, no possibility for fruitful conflict. Virgin and Dynamo have polar attributes, but they do not, cannot, interact. The power of the Virgin ran down and her influence died with the emergence, during the Renaissance, of the modern world. The power of the Dynamo is accelerating according to "the law of inverse squares" and will destroy us all. This power is curiously mortal, an emanation of Adams's own dissolving personality. He identified, in his intensely personal way, the end of his own life with the end of history. (And it might not be irrelevant to note that the chief prophets of cataclysmic philosophies of history—Carlyle, Spengler, Nietzsche, and Adams himself—were all childless men. Those who have not given hostages to Fortune can speculate with some comfort—and perhaps satisfaction—that the world will end with their deaths.)

Adams's view of history is anti-dialectical and linear. Unlike Hegel, who saw history as an immortal interchange of decay and growth, decline and progress, Adams saw steady decline toward ultimate chaos. Again unlike Hegel, Adams made no distinction between history and nature. Caught up in the Darwinism and Comtism of his age, he made a desperate subsumption of history under physics. Man and universe, action and thought, material cause and spiritual effect were lumped together as operating under the same putative law. History, nature, and human personality merged into a single substance impelled by the same energy. If the sun was destined to cool in two million (or billion) years, this to Adams was an omen of imminent historical disaster. If the laws of thermodynamics foretold a diminution of available energy in the universe, this to Adams meant certain historical catastrophe. Hegel noted that history is Spirit (human thought and action) moving through the realm of time; nature is "the development of the Idea in Space." Adams does not discriminate between nature, which displays cyclical, recurrent, and essentially predictable processes; and history, which displays ever renewed, ever different, cumulative, and spiraling processes.

Adams's linear eschatology and his analogical magic with the mathematics of doom issue from the Puritan imagination.

Adams's involuted, cranky sensibility, which often felt the events of history as personal outrages (or the machinations of the Jews), is a burden of New England character. His was, as Austin Warren points out, a New England conscience, fussily preoccupied with the state of the soul and dedicated to the pursuit of self-improvement. Adams does not escape Calvinist predestinarianism and its intoxication with types and symbols. Nor does Adams escape the New England agony of knowing that men are ordained to walk a certain path yet nevertheless must bear personal responsibility and endure the torments of guilt. Adams, like Gerontion, is caught in the Dynamo of historical process and confronted by History's bewildering power to confuse moral issues:

These tears are shaken from the wrath-bearing tree.

The power of History will destroy us; historical knowledge is at best fragmentary, incomplete; at worst, misleading. Caught in the process, deceived by knowledge: such was Henry Adams's dilemma. All the more agonizing was his emotional acceptance but intellectual rejection of the Christian solution to the historical riddle. He understood and approved the great medieval synthesis of religion, high culture, and common life—the supposed unity of thought and feeling which pervaded the age of the Gothic cathedrals. The intricate logic and aesthetic balance of medieval theology resolved the historical dilemma: history was a testing of souls in this world; its purpose and meaning became known in The City of God. But for Adams God had died with the advent of the modern world; and history, nature, and individual personality moved in a straight line to their destined conclusion.

III

T. S. Eliot

In all these occurrences and changes we behold human
action and suffering predominant; everywhere something
akin to ourselves, and therefore everywhere something that
excites our interest for or against. Sometimes it attracts us
by beauty, freedom, and rich variety; sometimes by energy
such as enables even vice to make itself interesting. Sometimes we see the more comprehensive mass of some general
interest advancing with comparative slowness, and subsequently sacrificed to an infinite complication of trifling
circumstances, and so dissipated into atoms. Then, again,
with a vast expenditure of power a trivial result is produced; while from what appears unimportant a tremendous
issue proceeds. On every hand there is the motliest throng
of events drawing us within the circle of its interest, and
when one combination vanishes another immediately appears in its place.

—Hegel, *The Philosophy of History*

GERONTION

I

In May 1919 T. S. Eliot reviewed *The Education of Henry
Adams* for *The Athenaeum* of London.[1] The review is de-
ceptively offhand, its tone patronizing and in places nearly
supercilious. Eliot regards Adams as a bright provincial
cousin: well-ancestored, well-connected, and well-heeled. Eliot
chides the New England character (which he knew well) for
its earnest dedication to self-improvement and portrays Adams
as "an elderly man approaching a new subject of study with

'This will be good for me!' " But Eliot's playful condescension and his portrait of Henry Adams as "little Paul Dombey asking questions" are rhetorical camouflage, the usual disguises of the Possum. *Gerontion,* the major poem of Eliot's 1920 collection (and one of the great poems of this century), echoes significant passages from *The Education.* Eliot compresses the lovely description from Chapter XVIII, "dogwood and the judastree, the azalea and the laurel . . . tulip and the chestnut . . . the . . . delicate grace and passionate depravity that marked the Maryland May" into a landscape for the violent advent of Christ the tiger:

In depraved May, dogwood and chestnut, flowering judas . . .

Other insistent music complements this borrowing. The ruined situation and wounded character of Gerontion, the prophetic voice of the poem, recall the elderly Adams with his broken neck and his prayers before the Dynamo. What breaks Adams's neck renders Gerontion blind and impotent. The concern in *Gerontion* is history as it is actually felt, a devastating force driving Europe toward cultural dissolution and moral despair; and history as it might be philosophically understood, a shattering Idea of History. This Idea leaves the protagonist incapable of action. However, Gerontion has lost only sight and passion; he retains his honesty. Though he meditates on history and predicts his own end in violence, he is no false prophet. His speculations, he insists, are not urged "by any concitation of the backward devils . . . ," by those who pry into the future for excitement or malign power. "The backward devils" are the legendary false prophets—soothsayers, fortune-tellers, necromancers—of Dante's fourth *bolgia* (*Inferno* XX). Their heads are twisted to the rear; their appropriate punishment is to gaze, with tear-filled eyes, eternally behind them. Remembering their torment, Gerontion pleads the rightness of his own motives for assuming the prophet's role. He does so neither for gain (like Madame Sosostris in *The Waste Land*), nor to dismay the credulous (like Madame de Tornquist in *Gerontion*). He tells us candidly:

I would meet you upon this honestly.

What does Gerontion meet us upon? It is the historical situation as seen by a nearly disembodied consciousness. Gerontion is blind, with gifts of foresight; he merges later with Tiresias in *The Waste Land.* His public experience is universal in space and time; his private life is apparently epicene. He dramatizes a complex of ideas about history and in one superb passage comments on the value of historical knowledge. These ideas, or more properly, speculations, are broadly philosophic; they touch on the senility of European culture, on the intolerable pressure of the past, and on the power and baffling direction of the historical process. Eliot is then, in *Gerontion,* a "philosopher of history": not because he gives a systematic account of historical process, but because he gives hints about the meaning and value of the past and views history as a dynamic, generating force. The poet as philosopher of history is also a prophet; he names things we have all felt and responded to: uncontrollable change, a fault below the structure of society, the transvaluation of values.

The opening of *Gerontion* is an astonishing compression of what Western civilization means in memory ("In memory only, reconsidered passion") to the old man. Gerontion was neither "at the hot gates"—Thermopylae, the archetypal scene of Greek heroism—nor "in the salt marsh, heaving a cutlass" in what seem to be Elizabethan wars of exploration. He has total recall; he was witness to the birth of Christ and he is a spectator at the downfall of the West. His personality merges with historical figures and with characters from the history of literature. He speaks with the words of Edward FitzGerald, the blind translator of the *Rubáiyát,* or in the iambic rhetoric of the Jacobean tragedians.

The pressure of this historical awareness paralyzes his capacity to act. We noted that Nietzsche denounced his contemporaries for overstressing the value of historical knowledge. The burdensome sense of the past is a malady of the modern world, leaving terrible scars on the individual personality and on the culture of nations. Gerontion cannot act because he cannot rid himself of his past; he too is an epigone, an injured victim of the historical sense. He believes in nothing; in a world dominated by history, matters for belief are bloodless reconstructions:

History . . . Gives too late
What's not believed in, or is still believed,
In memory only, reconsidered passion.

Gerontion "would see a sign," witness a rebirth of wonder
and belief, but historical knowledge has destroyed his capaci-
ties for sustaining illusion and giving assent. He knows too
much about the past of religion, about its anthropological
sources and its relation to primitive myth:

In the juvescence of the year
Came Christ the tiger . . .

Gerontion sees Christ as a culture hero who comes in the
season of the slain gods, when the flowering trees bloom.
Christ the tiger stalks us from the jungles of comparative
religion. Eliot suggests that religious growth needs fertile soil,
symbolized by lush vegetation and sexual activity. The tiger
is virile, potent; he recalls the other slain god Dionysus and
Nietzsche's description in *The Birth of Tragedy:* "The chariot
of Dionysus is bedecked with flowers and garlands; panthers
and tigers stride beneath his yoke." In contrast, Gerontion is
impotent, having "lost sight, smell, hearing, taste, and touch."

Nietzsche observed how the historical sense destroys the
religious sense; by knowing too much about a religion's past,
we come to recognize its absurdities and untruths. There can
be no passionate belief until history has been forgotten. The
participants in the obscure and sinister Communion, those
who have eaten and drunk Christ the tiger, are not communicants of a living, believed, and felt religion. Mr. Silvero,
Madame de Tornquist, Hakagawa, and Fräulein von Kulp
make ironic gestures toward what they know about the past.
Communion is not only the Christian ritual; it is also Eliot's
symbol for participation in Western culture and membership
in modern society. The names, suggesting the "international
set," underline the nature of the modern European world with
its disturbing juxtaposition of Spaniard and German, Gentile
and Jew, Oriental and Westerner. Society is international,
polyglot, and above all "historical."

Gerontion begins with an old man's reverie: a stream of
broken historical images and recollected meetings. With the
line "After such knowledge, what forgiveness?" Eliot drops

the dramatic mode and proposes, in a sustained didactic passage, an attitude toward history. The tone is hortatory; the argument, strengthened by a tightening of the metric and a repeated series of verbal motifs, has the "feel" if not the substance of logical discourse:

> *After such knowledge, what forgiveness? Think now*
> *History has many cunning passages, contrived corridors*
> *And issues, deceives with whispering ambitions,*
> *Guides us by vanities. Think now*
> *She gives when our attention is distracted*
> *And what she gives, gives with such supple confusions*
> *That the giving famishes the craving. Gives too late*
> *What's not believed in, or is still believed,*
> *In memory only, reconsidered passion. Gives too soon*
> *Into weak hands, what's thought can be dispensed with*
> *Till the refusal propagates a fear. Think*
> *Neither fear nor courage saves us. Unnatural vices*
> *Are fathered by our heroism. Virtues*
> *Are forced upon us by our impudent crimes.*
> *These tears are shaken from the wrath-bearing tree.*

Gerontion's knowledge is his obsessive, debilitating belief in the downfall of Europe. A mongrelized society and a polluted culture leave Gerontion little hope for regeneration; moral failure and religion known only in historical reconstruction point to little hope for spiritual rebirth. He waits for a terrifying development, a new and destructive display of historical energy. Like Henry Adams, he is prepared and even eager for violence: "The tiger springs in the new year. Us he devours."

But there is time to consider the past. What does historical knowledge tell about man's salvation? Very little, and this little dangerous:

> *Think now*
> *History has many cunning passages, contrived corridors*
> *And issues, deceives with whispering ambitions,*
> *Guides us by vanities*

"Think now": Gerontion urges us to an effort of will. He moves from reverie to intellectual commitment, to a position.

History is multiple: his personal past; an allegorized past, which is the history of Western culture from Thermopylae to the nineteenth century; and the immediate European present. Thus Madame de Tornquist and Mr. Silvero constitute a circle of shady acquaintances; "the hot gates" and "Christ the tiger" are moral and religious elements in Western culture; the Jew of Antwerp, Brussels, and London is scapegoat for all whose lives are international and uprooted. To Gerontion history is memory of the race, the memory of heroic action, the memory of his own symbolic past with its distressing lack of continuity.

Because history is so various, "has many cunning passages," it cannot be trusted to guide men in right action. History is female; her passages, corridors, and issues suggest both allurement and nausea. *Issues* are, of course, exits. They are also matters for dispute and decision—as in *political issues. An issue* may also be offspring or the discharge of bodily fluids. This cluster of meanings is heavily thematic, linking the motif of impotence and exacerbated sexuality to the emptiness of historical knowledge and the destructive whirlwind of historical process. The corridors of history are prepared and built; man's fate seems to be determined. Clio is his mistress and he is her fascinated yet reluctant lover. Doomed to haunt these corridors, he is misled by whispers and garbled voices, both tempted and dismayed by

> *Fräulein von Kulp*
> *Who turned in the hall, one hand on the door.*

But history itself cannot be blamed: the past means what Gerontion and men in general (for Gerontion's is the universal voice of prophecy) wish it to mean. Men manipulate the meaning of history to serve their moral comfort and suit their convenience. Urged by expediency and self-interest, deluded that they are instruments of the *Zeitgeist,* they make the appeal to History. They cry that their use of brute power is forced upon them by the intractable nature of events; they select, out of the bewildering experience of the past, examples necessary to justify their wickedness and rationalize their irresponsibility. Those who appeal to the inflexible nature of historical process and derive their moral values from the bloody record of the past are guided by vanities and distracted with supple confusion. For them, knowledge of the past is only the distorted image of themselves; the historical process becomes "manifest destiny," "the wave of the future," the avenging "Justice" of revolutionary terror.

> *Think now*
> *She gives when our attention is distracted*
> *And what she gives, gives with such supple confusions*
> *That the giving famishes the craving.*

What history gives is so devious, so subject to misinterpretation, that men finally give up in despair. They refuse her questionable generosity; her gifts no longer satisfy but create a more intense longing. Clio's seductive ways and motions starve the longing to know any more; many are reduced to Gerontion's helpless condition, losing "sight, smell, hearing, taste, and touch."

Gerontion's next imperative strengthens the notion that history is determined, impervious to individual action, whether for good or evil:

> *Think*
> *Neither fear nor courage saves us. Unnatural vices*
> *Are fathered by our heroism. Virtues*
> *Are forced upon us by our impudent crimes.*

The forces of history render the ethical will haphazard in action; men do the right things for the wrong reasons; deliberate evil may result in unexpected, unaccountable good. History has its own will which it makes known in an age of social violence and world war. Perhaps there has never been a time when individual man has felt himself so powerless before this will; he lives in an agony of events he abhors and faces values he can only regard with moral loathing. Gerontion is the protesting, apologetic voice of individual man in the grip of the historical process. He faces annihilation, yet would have his final say, "would meet you upon this honestly."

Gerontion's apology ends with an allusion to the Tree of the Knowledge of Good and Evil: "These tears are shaken from the wrath-bearing tree." Shaken, that is, from the ancestral branches of moral knowledge. In an age when the politician's daily appeal to history is the modern sin against the Holy Ghost, Gerontion raises embarrassing questions of good and evil and the responsibility of lonely, protesting men. Stemming from the Tree is the original loss of innocence past all forgiveness, the moral theme of Gerontion's apology. This passage, then, justifies the loss of Gerontion's innocence; but self-consciously, paradoxically, refuses the leading premise of its argument. The premise is that man is misled by History, that deluded and addled, he may evade the moral responsibilities of action and plead not guilty by reason of insanity. But there is no forgiveness; even though men will protest that they have been tricked by the cunning passages, confused by Clio's supple form, baffled by her dark declivities.

Earlier the polyglot communicants (Mr. Silvero, Hakagawa, Fräulein von Kulp) eat the body of Christ; now, in ironic retribution:

> *The tiger springs in the new year. Us he devours.*

The eaters are eaten. They had made an empty gesture (or perhaps a blasphemous one; Madame de Tornquist presides at some occult rite) of piety to propitiate a god believed "in memory only." Now the tiger devours what remains of a culture it once ("in the juvescence of the year") initiated. A "new year" suggests the start of a new historical cycle: Gerontion waits for the inevitable completion of the old era and the onslaught of the new. Eliot's Second Coming suggests a cyclical theory of history, some vision of Eternal Recurrence. Compare Eliot's tiger with Yeats's rough beast:

> *And what rough beast, its hour come round at last,*
> *Slouches towards Bethlehem to be born?*

Yeats's beast is not Christ. And in his second appearance the divine attributes of "Christ the tiger" seem overpowered by antithetical forces; the tiger becomes more purely tiger, an emblem of historical movement. Like the Dynamo and the rough beast, the tiger symbolizes irrational powers—forces moving the historical process. What fascinates is the sudden violence and relentless movement; history, despite its terrors, is at least life. History is energy, physical vitality.

Gerontion laments the loss of this energy. Speaking in the altered words of Beatrice, the lustful heroine of Thomas Middleton's *The Changeling,* he tells of adulterated passion and the need for artificial stimulations:

> *I that was near your heart was removed therefrom*
> *To lose beauty in terror, terror in inquisition.*
> *I have lost my passion: why should I need to keep it*
> *Since what is kept must be adulterated?*

The irony is that the hot-blooded Beatrice dies in a swirl of Renaissance violence; Gerontion, his senses decayed, stiffens in a rented house. In contrast to Beatrice and the other women and men of an age when passionate action was possible, Gerontion seeks perverse excitements. Beatrice was damned but she had the vitality of her sin. Gerontion, in his debility, must

> *Excite the membrane, when the sense has cooled,*
> *With pungent sauces, multiply variety*
> *In a wilderness of mirrors.*

The poem ends in a burst of cosmic power; it is total destruction. But Gerontion suggests that a new age is imminent; the turbulence at the end of the poem may proceed from a yet unknown, unnamed source of historical energy. Historical movement does not necessarily cease; civilization declines in the present chaos but the process continues:

> *Think at last*
> *We have not reached conclusion . . .*

Gerontion's personal annihilation in the whirlwind of history is a cause for remote hope. The death agonies of an old civilization may be the birth trauma of a new age. Gerontion is swept under the downward swirl of the Dialectic; but the rhythm may reverse and spiral outward toward "the new year." We think of Hegel at this point. Certainly Eliot gives hints and makes guesses that History is a transcendent, ceaseless process; that this process follows dialectical motions.

Gerontion once more apostrophizes the "international set" and the shabby boarders who share his house:

> *De Bailhache, Fresca, Mrs. Cammel, whirled*
> *Beyond the circuit of the shuddering Bear*
> *In fractured atoms.*

Through an Einsteinian metamorphosis these people are changed from mass to energy, their scattered substance blown by the cold winds of space. The end comes as a purgation, a clean sweep of the world and the old man's mind. The desire for annihilation is stressed. Since his world has grown so corrupt, Gerontion eagerly looks toward irrational force to destroy what remains of a decayed culture. As Adams gave up "the sequence of men," saw that "the sequence of society could lead no further," and attached himself to the principle of force, so Gerontion awaits the violence of history.

There are no explicit political meanings in *Gerontion*, but its cultural disillusion and millenarianism are omens of things to come. Eliot, through the mask of Gerontion, is saying his world has lost its moral moorings; bourgeois vulgarity and finance capitalism have made modern society impossible. Gerontion's world (the house of Europe) is in the hands of the Jews:

> *My house is a decayed house,*
> *And the Jew squats on the window sill, the owner . . .*[2]

Adams, we recall, shared this kind of economic anti-Semitism. In a letter to Charles Milnes Gaskell (1896), Adams fulminated, "Now no one doubts—and every Jew in London has acted on the belief—that America cannot maintain the gold standard . . . In the situation an investment is sheer gambling. We are in the hands of the Jews. They can do what they please with our values . . ."

The ugliness of such mouthings about Jews needs no particular underlining. Adams and Eliot saw the Jew as a symbol for historical decline, and although neither was a racist, their Judeophobia confirms Hannah Arendt's insight that "Doctrines of decay seem to have some very intimate connection with race-thinking."[3] Eliot was also, especially in the earlier years of his career, swayed by the doctrines of Charles Maurras. Maurras saw (in the social context of the Third Republic and the bitter aftermath of the Dreyfus Affair) the Jew as an eternal resident alien, the *métèque* who was unassimilable, incapable of national allegiance, and an excrescence on the body politic. The repulsive Jew, "spawned in some estaminet of Antwerp," emerges from the pages of *L'Action Française.*

Doctrines of decay and prophecies of violence are early symptoms of new political developments. The hope of disillusioned intellectuals—men like Maurras, Léon Daudet, and Barrès in France; Adams in America—lay in the destruction of the old society. They would help history along by attaching themselves to the principle of force; they showed no great nicety in advocating mob violence and racial hatred. Adams welcomed war as radical surgery for a sick civilization; Maurras emerging "from a ruinous and decadent cult of estheticism, saw in the mob a living expression of virile and primitive 'strength.' "[4] Eliot long maintained an ambivalent attitude toward the politics of blood and soil; he strained hard to hear "the wave of the future": "the peculiar note of breakers on a reef. This note . . . is of authority not democracy, of dogmatism not tolerance, of the extremity and never of the mean."[5] What is intimated in *Gerontion*—philosophic pessimism, dreams of apocalypse, anti-Semitism, Nietzschean *amor fati*— affords a prophetic glimpse into the desperate political programs of the coming era.

Eliot cautions us that Gerontion's views are provisional, tentative, or even the product of a disturbed mind. Almost as a disclaimer, as a note of deprecating explanation comes Gerontion's final address to his contemporaries (Madame de Tornquist, Mr. Silvero, *et al.*):

> *Tenants of the house*
> *Thoughts of a dry brain in a dry season.*

Gerontion's mind may be disordered, but he knows that salvation is not found in past and present. Gerontion dramatizes the dynamics of history but Eliot, like Adams of *The Education,* distrusts the value of historical knowledge. After the Jew of Antwerp and Brussels, after the necromancy of Madame de Tornquist, and the temptations of Fräulein von Kulp, what forgiveness indeed? Historical process is real and terrifying; historical knowledge is stale passion and supple confusion. We are brought back to our controlling paradox. Modern man is up to his neck in events, overwhelmed by historical process; but the records of the past, history in its epistemological sense, can provide no moral examples, no safe pattern for action, no program for an ethical politics.

It is this controlling paradox which gives *Gerontion* its dialectical vigor and sweeping urgency. Eliot sees events more or less forced upon the protesting individual; man struggles in the web of circumstance, unable to act for himself. Such is Gerontion's situation and the situation of the age he symbolizes. Gerontion dreams and remembers; sexual activity and political action are both beyond his feeble powers. His mind (or what remains of it) holds an extreme past and an extreme present. This present is what Gerontion thinks the modern world is like. We may think the modern world has more to offer than the sycophancy of Hakagawa and the come-on of Fräulein von Kulp. We may believe that although the possibilities for action are limited, they are not completely closed. Eliot certainly dramatizes in *Gerontion* a deterministic interpretation of the historical process; the poem supports, in its imagery and rhetoric, a Spenglerian *Schicksalsidee*. Yet any strongly expressed attitude toward history, any considered awareness of the meaning of events moves towards determinism. Technical philosophies of history are, almost by definition, "deterministic" in that they see man's life in time as tragically limited.

Eliot's moral sense intrudes upon the spectacular performance of modern history. Though men are at the mercy of history—its deceits and false hopes—they are responsible for their actions, guilty of their crimes. Eliot invokes virtue and vice and uses these creaking terms in a startlingly corrosive context. Virtue and vice are still moral imperatives. Under the double burden of ethical responsibility and historical necessity men are reduced to Gerontion's debilitated condition. In another time this might have been the situation for tragedy. But Gerontion cannot defy fate (or History), succumb gloriously, and thereby assert the dignity and freedom of the human spirit. He declines in impotence and hopes for extinction.

To be denied the freedom of the will and yet be held to moral responsibility is the by now familiar Existential projection of the human dilemma: Calvinism without the feeble light of grace illuminating the obscure path to salvation. But we must remember that poetry makes capital out of such impossibilities, that Eliot is dramatizing, not dogmatizing. We have been able to isolate certain attitudes because Eliot's method in *Gerontion* is general and allegorical; it is a vision of the world and human destiny two years after the First World War.

That Eliot's vision is projected through an old blind prophet dreaming on heroic action and other people's sex lives, that Gerontion is reduced to madness by his sensitivity to the corruption and futility of his age, attest to the critical importance with which Eliot regards the historical process. Eliot is acutely aware of the dynamism of history: as aware as any political revolutionary inflamed by pathological sensitivity to the *Zeitgeist*. In their historical objectivity, both *Gerontion* and *The Waste Land* remain brilliant critical assessments of modern culture. Eliot holds a "historicist" position; man is a product of historical development, totally determined by an unredeemed past and a chaotic present. Indeed, Eliot sees history through Hegelian lenses, and attributes to the great sweep of action and event dialectical movement, exultant energy and the paradoxical permanence of ceaseless change. However, Eliot cautions against the Hegelian error (more precisely, the error of Hegelians) of compounding the examples of history into an expedient morality. What happened in history was not necessarily right. *Gerontion* teems with the images, instances, and recollections of the multitudinous past; Eliot knows that such knowledge stems from the wrath-bearing tree.

THE WASTE LAND

2

The Waste Land never ceases to be a prophecy fulfilled. What once seemed a hallucinated unfolding of transformations and horrors and a botched work of art, whose shapelessness imitated its thematic incoherence, is now a familiar access to reality. Its "towers/Tolling reminiscent bells . . ." shadow the polluted urban landscape in which we gasp for breath. We need only drive through the surrounding megalopolis, rehearse the pressures of our growing up, and compute the odds for survival to "understand" Eliot's meanings. Of course, like all influential works of literature, *The Waste Land* continually enters the collective imagination and the common language. We hear weather reports commenting on the rainiest and cruelest month; the Greater Trumps of the Tarot appear as characters in low-brow fiction and cheap movies; Fisher Kings and Hyacinth Girls turn up on the fringes of both the middle class and the newest version of Bohemia. Life *will* imitate art; or, more precisely, catches up with it.

Because we know it so well, it may seem odd, or perhaps simple-minded to ask (fifty years and fifty books later) what *The Waste Land* is "about." Any number of answers, buttressed by formidable theorizing, are available. We may learn that *The Waste Land,* quite simply, is about itself; it is a closed aesthetic world and its meanings refer back to its self-sufficient contextual unity. Or *The Waste Land* embodies (or, more theologically, *incarnates*) the universal myth of seasonal renewal, the eternal suffering of gods ritually slain and reborn. These are familiar answers: immensely useful, invaluable. Such has been the influence and utility of modern scholarship that the meaning of *The Waste Land* is now inextricably bound up with the meanings exacted by its criticism. Murray Krieger's striking metaphor for the ontology of the poem can help here.[6] A poem is both mirror and window: its structures reflect the act of its creation; it also looks out upon the world, to "history and existence." If we agree that *The Waste Land* is a mirror reflecting the complexities of its own structure and natural process, it is also a window through which we view a scene dense with social life and writhing with agonized human concern.

The chief spectator at this window is the prophet Tiresias, the enlarged and multiplied persona of *Gerontion*. Tiresias emerges "the most important personage in the poem, uniting all the rest . . . What Tiresias *sees*, in fact, is the substance of the poem."[7] From the deadly stability of his ruin, Gerontion watches (in his mind's eye, for he is blind) De Bailhache and Mrs. Cammel; hears, in adjacent rooms, Mr. Silvero and Fräulein von Kulp. But Tiresias *melts into,* becomes all the other characters in *The Waste Land.* We pass the boundaries of *Gerontion* and enter a more populous though nonetheless stifling world—where Tiresias marvels: "I had not thought death had undone so many."

The central, suffering consciousness of Tiresias unites *The Waste Land;* his voice, disguised in a series of brilliant impersonations, is always identifiable by its moral intensity, by its rhythms which are attitudes. We recall that *The Waste Land* is meant as an objective poem: in accordance with Eliot's critical theory, a classical release from personal emotion and romantic self-indulgence. Yet this "classical" poem speaks in varying inflections of hysteria and catatonic indifference. Indeed, it is through tone of voice, through sound and timbre, that *The Waste Land* approaches coherence. The poem's aesthetic surface—its carrying metric and extraordinarily musical syntax—provides a more essential ground of unity than mythic pattern or thematic symbolism. Hearing Eliot read *The Waste Land* solves the "obscurity" of its meaning and structure. The voice of *The Waste Land* is as unmistakable, as personal, as the voice of *The Prelude.* The vision in *The Waste Land* possesses the objectivity of all Romantic vision; Eliot's History, like Wordsworth's Nature, is shaped by the imagination of a poet who is his own hero.

Gerontion speaks to the unsavory "Tenants of the house . . .": the manipulators, feather-merchants, and demi-mondaines who throng an uncertain space between sordid actuality and failing memory. Tiresias also speaks to the deceived and the deranged, the fraudulent and the impotent; he assumes a minatory stance and utters the thunder of The Authorized Version:

> *Son of man*
> *You cannot say, or guess, for you know only*
> *A heap of broken images, where the sun beats,*
> *And the dead tree gives no shelter, the cricket no relief . . .*

If Gerontion is one man registering his protest, Tiresias, in becoming all the men and women of *The Waste Land,* is modern historical awareness. *The Waste Land* enlarges Gerontion's impassioned polemic that the will cannot save men from History and its terrible exactions on knowledge and commitment. History is re-enacted, not in its ruthless dynamism, but in its frozen moments. We encounter history recalled: the exemplary past which is more often mocked and parodied than praised or treated with nostalgia. We encounter the problematic present, the world of perpetual crisis. We are vouchsafed a vision of the future, the apocalypse to come. The poem apprehends a revolution already in progress and bloody disasters looming on the horizon. And the whole mode of apprehension is traditionally prophetic: that is to say, profoundly moral. The voice of Tiresias trembles in unequivocal didactic passion. He condemns the present in a series of sordid revelations; he reminds us that the past is unredeemable and the source of our present miseries; he sees the future in the violet air, which illuminates in eerie synaesthesia, the downfall of cities:

> *Falling towers*
> *Jerusalem Athens Alexandria*
> *Vienna London*
> *Unreal*

The reader is not spared. By collapsing all characters into one character, *The Waste Land* establishes a close relationship with the reader and renders every experience accessible in an almost embarrassingly intimate way. Tiresias, in the guise of a mordant and melancholy voyeur, observes the coldblooded fornication of a pimply real estate clerk and a bored typist. We squirm, not because of the clumsy and loveless sexual encounter, but because we have "perceived the scene" through the frozen lust of a Peeping Tom. The scene offers an objective correlative for emotions we do not enjoy sharing, but we cannot deny the effectiveness of Eliot's procedures.

Other virtuosities reenforce other meanings. The manipulation of sequence and progression, essentially a compositional device or even gimmick, acts out an attitude toward history. Everything that "happens" in *The Waste Land* happens on the same temporal plane; the poem has no narrative before and after. The visit to Madame Sosostris and the evocation of Gethsemane ("the agony in stony places") occur simultaneously. Every episode, from the first scene in a Munich café ("Summer . . . coming over the Starnbergersee") to the lonely fisherman ("with the arid plain behind") shoring fragments against ruin, is still going on when the poem concludes. Eliot, like Pound in the *Cantos,* banishes chronology. Past and present become phantasmagoric, surreal; often we cannot be sure whether an experience is actual or imagined, whether it is realized in action or recollected in hallucinated tranquility. April mingles memory and desire, the epistemological and the ontological, until the protagonists despair of both knowledge and action. A woman cries to her lover:

> "Do
> "You know nothing? Do you see nothing? Do you remember
> "Nothing?"

After the emptiness of knowledge, there can only be the twitch of the organism, action which is mere behavior:

> "What shall I do now? What shall I do?"
> "I shall rush out as I am, and walk the street
> "With my hair down, so. What shall we do tomorrow?
> "What shall we ever do?"

History, our corrupt and partial knowledge, is entangled with our will; history becomes the extremity of action, the final heave of the process.

Which brings our point to bear against the substance of *The Waste Land.* In *Gerontion* the process, imaged in the exultant energy of the tiger and the fracturing winds, presents itself as an imminent possibility. In *The Waste Land* the process has all but stopped; the great dynamo of change has been short-circuited. Here and there we observe movement without purpose: dirty hands grasp at nothing; eyes stare down at the ground, unwilling to meet other eyes; sullen faces sneer and snarl. All motion is embarrassed. Madame Sosostris sees ". . . crowds of people, walking round in a ring." (They walk in that stale hell, the chartered city, whose center is a slum and whose circumference cuts the middle-class suburbs.) We are suspended in time; the characters all wait for some expected event. The bartender's voice in "A Game of Chess" cries in urgent capitals:

HURRY UP PLEASE ITS TIME

but time has curved in upon itself; history waits and nothing happens.

Eliot's copy of Jessie Weston's *From Ritual to Romance,* now in Harvard's Houghton Library, contains a few uncut pages. Its generally virgin appearance and its lack of marginal annotations indicates it was not the object of overly serious perusal. Of course, Eliot probably read enough to serve his purpose—which was that of the poet and not the scholar. *From Ritual to Romance* provides no immediate key to *The Waste Land;* indeed Eliot has teased those exegetes who accepted his notes to the poem at face value and then discovered they had been "sent . . . off on a wild goose chase after Tarot cards and the Holy Grail."[8] *The Golden Bough,* Arthurian myth, and primitive ritual are necessary parts of the poem; but do they not function (to recall one of Eliot's analogies) as the meat which the burglar throws the watchdog? The critic falls hungrily on the poet's learning and skill in arranging recondite materials; the poet meanwhile goes stealthily about his felonious business. The critics of myth and symbol have dealt not with the poem's substance but largely with its surface technique.

The substance of *The Waste Land* is not ahistorical or antihistorical myth but history as it might be philosophically understood. (Eliot's copy of Hegel's *The Philosophy of History,* which he owned as a Harvard undergraduate, contains no uncut pages; it does contain numerous annotations and underlinings. He obviously read it from cover to cover.) Inherent in the symbolism of *The Waste Land* and embodied in its patterns of ritual and archetype, are the confused phenomena we may recognize as history, and speculation on the possible meaning of what we think we see. The historical situation is dramatized by a series of sexual encounters alternating with moments of religious expectation. *The Waste Land* is "about" history and how it affects making love; it is "about" those prophetic moments between the Crucifixion and the Resurrection: after the end and before the beginning. During those moments Tiresias waits for history to resume, to begin again with a new dispensation. In the interim, while the process is suspended, men and women pursue patterns of despair and circular madness. The sexual encounters are failures of potency, mechanical copulations, and moments recalled in ecstasy and guilt:

> *The awful daring of a moment's surrender*
> *Which an age of prudence can never retract*
> *By this, and this only, we have existed . . .*

The sentiment here is Jamesian; it evokes Strether's injunction to live life to the fullest and enter passionately into relationships with others—for how else can we know we have been here and left our mark on the present? But like Strether, the protagonist of *The Waste Land* grasps intellectually what he cannot himself put into action.

The poem opens with the sudden shock of seasonal renewal; April stirs the protagonist to painful feelings of new hopes and new responses. The *mise en scène* is middle European, the locale precisely designated:

> *Summer surprised us, coming over the Starnbergersee . . .*

Lake Starnberg is near Munich, a city heavy with nineteenth-century decadence and an artistic past dominated by Richard Wagner and his strange patron, Ludwig II of Bavaria. The "voice" in the opening lines is a woman's; the single voice immediately melts into a babble of overheard conversation. We are in the Hofgarten, now serving as a café for polyglot tourists. From the next table another woman protests, with unconscious ironic self-contradiction, that she is not a Russian but a genuine German from Lithuania. She is obviously a Jewess, one of Europe's perennial aliens, pretending to a nationality she does not rightfully possess. The voice of another woman recalls *un instant de puissance et de délire:*

> *And when we were children, staying at the arch-duke's,*
> *My cousin's, he took me out on a sled,*
> *And I was frightened. He said, Marie,*
> *Marie, hold on tight. And down we went.*

(To George L. K. Morris this episode suggests Hapsburg intrigue. In a half-spoofing article he identifies Marie as one

Countess Marie Larisch and the archduke cousin as Rudolph, son of the Emperor Franz Josef and heir to the Austro-Hungarian throne.[9])

After the prophetic tirade which threatens fear in a handful of dust, Eliot introduces the sailor's song from the opening of *Tristan und Isolde:*

> *Frisch weht der Wind*
> *Der Heimat zu*
> *Mein Irisch Kind*
> *Wo weilest du?*

The ditty not only remembers Wagner's most celebrated lovers but also suggests how Wagnerian techniques and Wagnerism in general enter *The Waste Land.* Later we hear the voices of the Thames Maidens set to the *Rheingold* music; we also hear, in a grotesque context, the chorus of Grail Knights from *Parsifal:*

> *Et O ces voix d'enfants, chantant dans la coupole!*

The line is from Verlaine's poem *Parsifal.* The entire French Symbolist movement was saturated in Wagnerian theory and *die Musik der Zukunft.* That the memory of Wagner should haunt a poem that established Symbolist theory and practice as a modern tradition is hardly strange.

We note a train of association: a Hapsburg archduke, *mitteleuropäische* corruption, and Wagner's two "decadent" operas—*Tristan und Isolde,* which tells an overheated tale of love and death; and *Parsifal,* which makes a plea for Aryan racial purity in the ambiance of a Black Mass. Indeed, *The Waste Land* picks up some of that perverse religiosity which pervades Wagner's *fin-de-siècle* retelling of the medieval myth of quest and redemption. It may also be worth noting that orchestrated into the score of *The Waste Land* is "the death by water" motif; it was in Lake Starnberg that King Ludwig drowned. (Like the deaths of the Archduke Rudolph and Mary Vetsera, Ludwig's suicide has been questioned; some say Wagner's eccentric patron was the victim of an elaborate Prussian *Putsch.*)

The song from *Tristan* is prelude to a laconic interchange

between the Hyacinth Girl and the male protagonist. He is despondent; like Prufrock he has been unable to speak, unable to ask the overwhelming question which will elicit responsive love. The girl was more than ready; stimulated and submissive, she was open to the masculine gesture:

Your arms full, and your hair wet . . .

Yet the man turns away; once again knowledge and action fail. He can only stare in embarrassed silence; he cannot make love because

Between the desire
And the spasm
Between the potency
And the existence
Between the essence
And the descent
Falls the Shadow.

Another, more explicit encounter between unhappy lovers expands the brief agony of The Hyacinth Girl and her ineffectual Tristan. In "A Game of Chess," amid aristocratic decor and Baroque splendor, a woman threatens to run disheveled and mad through the city streets. She taxes her lover (or husband) with an age-old female complaint:

"Speak to me. Why do you never speak . . ."

She implores her lover to tell her that she is alive; he mocks her with macabre or irrelevant replies:

I think we are in rats' alley
Where the dead men lost their bones.

Like The Hyacinth Girl she languishes in sexual need; she will offer herself in the city streets:

"I shall rush out as I am, and walk the street
"With my hair down, so. . . .

Eliot displays some decided Victorian preferences for long hair and equates it with sexual availability.

The second part of "A Game of Chess" is located in the ladies' salon of a London pub. To emphasize that the malaise on love afflicts both high and low, we overhear a cockney woman deliver an "I said . . . she said" monologue. She reports a conversation between herself and a woman who is not present, "Poor Lil." Poor Lil has taken drugs to abort an unwanted child:

> *It's them pills I took, to bring it off, she said . . .*
> *The chemist said it would be all right, but I've never*
> *been the same.*

The monologist displays no womanly compassion for Lil but thinks her a fool:

> *What you get married for if you don't want children?*

It is hard to miss the general nastiness directed toward women in *The Waste Land*. In Eliot's recording of the poem, he reads the final line of "A Game of Chess" (". . . good night, *sweet* ladies, good night. . . .") with a meaningfully ironic stress on *sweet* and an undisguised valedictory sneer.

"The Fire Sermon" is the longest section of the poem and forms a center of emphasis. It is here that the motif of sterile lust is fully developed and reaches a *stretto* in the perfunctory seduction of the typist. Tiresias appears in his androgynous role,

> *. . . throbbing between two lives,*
> *Old man with wrinkled female breasts . . .*

and reports the homosexual solicitation of Mr. Eugenides as well as the episode between "the young man carbuncular" and his bored ladyfriend. This episode is recounted in leisurely detail, in deliberate, rhymed pentameters. The eye of Tiresias (the masturbatory eye of the voyeur) picks up articles of female clothing, the disorder of the young woman's poorly furnished lodgings, and the harsh emptiness of her life.

A musical transition links the typist with the three Thames maidens. The blare of "the record on the gramophone" mingles with the strings and sweet sounds of Prospero's island:

> *"This music crept by me upon the waters"*

A walk "along the Strand, up Queen Victoria Street" brings the reader "Beside a public bar in Lower Thames Street" where we hear other music, "The pleasant whining of a mandoline . . ." All this modulatory preparation leads into the music of the Thames Maidens who parody the song of Wagner's three Rhine Daughters:

> *Weialala leia*
> *Wallala leialala*

At the Thames's edge the three maidens retell the shame and numb acceptance of their respective seductions. Like the cockney women in "A Game of Chess" and the errant typist, they are lower-class victims of male aggression. The maidens are submissive; their fate is the expected fate of "humble people who expect/Nothing." The marks of their class are

> *The broken fingernails of dirty hands . . .*

Near the end of Part V, "What the Thunder Said," the protagonist again encounters The Hyacinth Girl or her psychological counterpart.

> Damyata: *The boat responded*
> *Gaily, to the hand expert with sail and oar*
> *The sea was calm, your heart would have responded*
> *Gaily, when invited, beating obedient*
> *To controlling hands . . .*

Her heart *would have responded,* her body would have obeyed the hand "expert with sail and oar." But the implication is that the hand kept to its proper business; at the critical moment the protagonist lost his nerve and made no gesture. A certain prudence may have inhibited the protagonist; lovemaking in an open boat has its dangers. However, such consideration did not restrain the foolhardy lover of the first Thames Maiden who took his girl

> *Supine on the floor of a narrow canoe.*

This selective summary shows how much the poem is obsessed with frustrated sexuality and encounters which are little more than rapes. The attitudes toward sex are Manichean; the body arouses both desire and disgust: the protagonist burns with Augustine in the cauldrons of unholy lust. But the curse on human love, on sharing affection and losing identity, does not issue only from the anguished Jansenism of Eliot's personality. Modern life and the pressures of history have contrived to throw dirt on love. "That dirty war" and an enervating peace have rendered men either impotent or brutally lustful and women either hysterical or frigidly acquiescent. The situation is polarized and we again think of the Virgin and the Dynamo. The creative powers have been destroyed; the irrational forces of History have not only broken necks but strangled the desire to reproduce the species. The copulations are indifferent events; if the women conceive, they abort their children.

History as the immediate past looms behind the men and women of *The Waste Land;* the First World War and its four years of senseless blood-letting are involved in even the most private neurosis. Behind the immediate past stretches the totality of history, from primitive *ur*-existence to a noise in the street. And mingled with the noises of the street, with children chanting "London Bridge is falling down," comes an embarrassed disclaimer which echoes Gerontion's final apology. A voice cries, as if it meant to caution the reader not to take what he has read too seriously, "Hieronymo's mad againe." Eliot knows the prophetic role is equivocal; it carries a desperate responsibility, and those who undertake it must not forget the possible "concitation/Of the backward devils."

Early interpreters of *The Waste Land* gave us a sense of the poem's richness and mystery. They dug up fragments, shards of vessels long since shattered. The quest for the Grail and its attendant fertility rituals, however, forms no heuristic pattern: nothing to which the mind can attach itself in discovery. Even if we understand the Grail Myth as a sub-plot which tells what is taking place in the upper narrative, we are not satisfied. But if we interpret "myth" to mean in Eliot's context a metahistorical search for meaning in human events, it is then possible to say *The Waste Land* suspends us between the two major myths explaining the shape of historical processes. Eliot pauses in a moment of suspended history to consider alternative metahistorical fictions.

These fictions are rendered in religious symbology. We can read *The Waste Land* as a sacred text, a typological book to be interpreted backwards and forwards. It looks back to Eliot's early poems of alienation and urban despair and ahead to his poems of explicit Christian experience. It also involves us with the myth of Buddha and Hindu metaphysics; it strives toward the obliteration of consciousness and the peace which passeth understanding. The search for The Hanged Man, the agony in stony places, and the sense that the entire poem takes place between the Crucifixion and the Resurrection suggest a Christian explanation to the problem of history. (I would, at this point, wish to regard Eliot's symbology as indication of his metahistorical assumptions rather than as intimation of his conversion.) Part V, "What The Thunder Said," begins in a long moment of prophetic expectation. The time is after the Crucifixion:

> *After the torchlight red on sweaty faces*
> *After the frosty silence in the gardens*
> *After the agony in stony places*

Christ has not yet entered history; the corpse in the garden has not yet bloomed.

But Eliot hesitates before another possibility which contradicts the Christian belief in a rectilinear historical process and the Pauline exhortation that "Christ raised from the dead dieth no more." Part V, with its Sanskrit invocation and closing benediction glances toward ancient India and eastern concepts of historical cycles. The mingling of the myths of Osiris and Adonis with the myth of The Hanged God Who Shall Live Again indicates that Eliot was thinking of Christianity as another fertility cult whose rituals and beliefs were founded in the eternal cycle of the seasons.

The sense that history is eternally recurrent is strongest in the last section of *The Waste Land*. A new source of energy appears in the east. Spengler saw the shock waves of history moving from east to west and Hegel noted that "The History of the World travels from East to West, for Europe is absolutely the end of History, Asia the beginning."[10] (Hegel, in his dialectical way, denied the circularity of history while also affirming the end of History in Europe and its subsequent continuation in America.) Eliot acknowledges the new push from Asia and "the present decay of Eastern Europe" in a vision of refugees fleeing war and revolution:

> *What is that sound high in the air*
> *Murmur of maternal lamentation*
> *Who are those hooded hordes swarming*
> *Over endless plains, stumbling in cracked earth*
> *Ringed by the flat horizon only . . .*

Eliot glosses these lines with a passage from Hermann Hesse:

> By this time half of Europe—at least half of Eastern Europe—is on the way to chaos, traveling in holy drunken madness along the edge of the abyss, and singing as it goes along, singing drunkenly and hymn-like as Dmitri Karamazov sang. The insulted citizen laughs at these songs; the saint and prophet hear them with tears.

This passage is taken from Hesse's essay, "The Brothers Karamazov, or the Downfall of Europe."[11] Hesse reads Dostoevsky's novel as a prophecy of the downfall of the west; the madness of the Karamazovs is not a matter for literary criticism but for cultural diagnosis and speculation on the nature of historical process. Dostoevsky is named *genius loci* of the European downfall; he does not suffer a private illness or merely dream psychotic visions: "the nightmare which oppresses him does not warn him of his own sickness, of a personal death, but of the body whose organ and antenna he is. This may be a family, a party, a people—it may be all mankind."

For Hesse the onslaught of the Karamazovs, which heralds the European downfall, does not generate historical pessimism but rather new hopes. The ideal of the Karamazovs, imaged in a downward journey, "a return home to the Mother, a turning back to Asia, to the Faustian mothers . . . will obviously lead, like every death on earth, to a new birth." The conclusion of *The Waste Land,* with its "Murmur of maternal lamentation," hints that a cultural renewal may issue from familiar sources. We are reminded that both the gods of the fertility rites and the God of Israel emerged from Asia. *The Waste Land* relives, in the image of the withered Sybil of Cumae, the first century of the Roman Empire when the ancient world was unsuc-

cessfully resisting the invasions of new and apparently destructive forces. Unknown to the Romans of their age, these
were forces of spiritual renewal and historical rebirth.

Eliot, however, entertains historical renewal only as a
possibility. *The Waste Land* envisions man barely surviving the
miseries of modern civilization; the protagonist does not break
through to a new cultural, historical, or religious dimension.
We sense, of course, the struggle *to break through*. Characters
reach out for some ungraspable proffered hand; but they make
gestures that elicit no communal response. They live their
lives between hysteria and oblivion without the passion of
belief. What is left to them are violent dreams and a residuum
of physical disgust. The emphasis on sexuality seems the final
spasm of a waning ascetic culture; the culture has long ago
relinquished its claim to a viable public philosophy in its un-
critical acceptance of private moralities. It is a culture prac-
ticing an aggressively futile non-attachment. And the resulting
polity is what we now experience in the credibility gaps yawn-
ing between the realities of power and the fragments we shore
against ruin. What we know are broken images, the lies
and simulacra which hold together the semblance of a living
culture.

FOUR QUARTETS

3

Gerontion and *The Waste Land* confront a world heavy with
unredeemed time. History-littered landscapes, copious use of
ironic literary allusion, the parodic treatment of myth—all
weave a thick texture of present and remembered event. Obsessed with history, these earlier poems end *pianissimo* on unresolved chords of tentative apocalyptic speculation. The structural sequence concluding both *Gerontion* and *The Waste
Land* is identical. A number of images drawn from the
natural world—the springing tiger, the gull in the whirlwind,
thunder and rain over the Himalayas—stimulate expectation
that we shall witness some spectacular conclusion to history.
But neither the tiger nor the gull awakes Gerontion from his
after-dinner sleep; he complains of brain fatigue. The Sanskrit-

speaking thunder and rain do nothing to alleviate the drought of *The Waste Land;* the protagonist, like Gerontion, questions his mental competence. Historical energy has run down so that even the apocalypse is aborted:

> *This is the way the world ends*
> *Not with a bang but a whimper.*

In *Four Quartets* the concern with history, with concrete event, the memory of the past, and the powerful "sequence of force," changes into something more metaphysically ordered and more deeply theoretical. The horror of History, imaged in the springing tiger or the dead wall of the contrived corridor, gives way to Christian theodicy. Historical process, exacting its price in human suffering, is emblematic and redemptive. To the instructed, certain moments "in and out of time" point to a reality more crucially significant than the undifferentiated stream of events we ordinarily call history. Passages of intellectual thrust and parry, of dialectic, directly consider the value of historical knowledge; speculate that such knowledge may or may not be useful for human salvation; and tell us that historical process, moving toward a divinely established goal outside of human history, is understandable only to the extent that God allows us to understand it.

These are obviously Christian explanations and solutions to the problem of history—insofar as poetry obliges with bluebook information or comforts with solutions. The Christian elements in the *Quartets* contribute richly to their thematic structure and enhance their metaphoric grandeur. The basic plot moves from prelapsarian innocence, symbolized by the Rose Garden episode in "Burnt Norton," through the lesson of history which is suffering, to final acceptance of God's will in this world and hope for Grace in the next. However, *Four Quartets* resembles neither a versified homily nor traditional poems of Christian theodicy and Christian devotion; *Four Quartets* is a meditative poem employing a varied philosophic method designed to explore and mediate between Christian belief and existential possibility.

Let me note that I do not always find Eliot's Christianity congenial. It is conceived on a narrow base; Eliot's attempt to justify the ways of God to men is deficient in evangelical warmth and love for God's created beings. Earlier we spoke of "the anguished Jansenism of Eliot's personality." Jansenism stresses the radical corruption of man; life is an ordeal of suffering and expiation in a world of inherited evil:

> *The whole earth is our hospital*
> *Endowed by the ruined millionaire,*
> *Wherein, if we do well, we shall*
> *Die of the absolute paternal care . . .*

The ruined millionaire is Adam who lost his inheritance through Original Sin. History exists to administer man's ongoing penance:

> *The one discharge from sin and error.*
> *The only hope, or else despair*
> *   Lies in the choice of pyre or pyre—*
> *To be redeemed from fire by fire.*

Men accept their penance or are damned. Eliot may be saying no more than that human life entails suffering and the Purgatory of history refines moral sensibilities. But there is a punitive sharpness to Eliot's moral probings; in some moods (as in the nearly hysterical *After Strange Gods*) his Jansenist attitudes generate distinct totalitarian overtones. Eliot was no fascist; he was both too decent and too prudent. But his attachments during the late twenties and thirties to rigidly structured social schemes, to the idea of an authoritarian church, and to political desperadoes like Charles Maurras, brought him close to the extreme right. If one deeply believes that human existence is ordained as retribution for Original Sin, it is easy to accept (even welcome) repressive and punitive political systems.

The darkest illumination of the *Quartets* streams from Eliot's estimation of man's fallen nature. Eliot early rejected the humanist belief that man was the measure of all things:

> (*The lengthened shadow of a man*
> *   Is history, said Emerson*
> *Who had not seen the silhouette*
> *   Of Sweeney straddled in the sun.*)
>   "Sweeney Erect" (1920)

The history of Sweeney and his friends is a sordid tale, not to be dignified with the honorific *history*. Eliot corrects Emerson, so notably deficient in a sense of radical evil, for his liberal and progressive doctrines; and it is true that Emerson preferred not to think about the Sweeneys and Mrs. Turners of this world. No inhabitant of Sweeney's milieu obtrudes upon the *Quartets;* Eliot's attention turns toward mediation between historical existence and the City of God, between time and eternity. Eliot accepts without exultation the limitations that bind men to their essential humanity (which must include their animality). One path of the *Quartets* runs through Eliot's familiar half-world of death-in-life. "Burnt Norton" returns to London, The Unreal City: "Men and bits of paper . . ." flutter in a dim light across windswept hills. In "East Coker" the humble and great pass into darkness; and we learn that "There is . . . /At best, only a limited value/In the knowledge derived from experience." Eliot reiterates the old lesson that men learn little, if anything, from history. Nor does the process perform a useful therapy: "Time is no healer: the patient is no longer here . . ." In "Little Gidding" Eliot's "familiar compound ghost" rehearses the grim platitude, in Dantesque language that is scarcely platitudinous, that man's temporal journey ends in the debility and frustration of old age:

> *First, the cold friction of expiring sense . . .*
> *And last, the rending pain of re-enactment*
> *Of all that you have done and been . . .*

Perhaps I overstress Eliot's sombre vision and his concern with the disappointment of human hopes. The humanist (whether Marxist or liberal) may still prefer to dream that man, through his own efforts, will move toward happier modes of personal and social existence. But the vision of a declining secular culture, projected in all Eliot's work, has scarcely been disconfirmed by recent history. Many of our most sensitive social prophets now insist, as did the author of *The Idea of a Christian Society,* that no culture can flourish without deep spiritual commitments and that the cultural crisis of our age is a religious crisis. Doubtless Eliot's understanding of history, insofar as that understanding emerges as personal Christian eschatology, serves only his own salvation. (It is cold comfort for Eliot to promise that in heaven "All manner of things will be well. . . .") Those of us unsustained by Christian hope, impelled by new urgencies and terrorized by the threat of a new apocalypse, must redeem the time in different ways. Yet nothing Eliot says about the meaning of history is without existential relevance. Christian theodicy and Christian understanding of the redemptive possibilities of the historical process can be "demythologized" and their supernatural promises be translated into secular hopes. Our salvation *from* history (whether we are liberals, traditionalists, or Marxists) follows a torturous path *through* history; our freedom from the tyranny of time can only be won on the battle line of the temporal process. "Only through time time is conquered."

The opening lines of "Burnt Norton" define, in language at once paradoxical and colorless, the temporal flux:

> *Time present and time past*
> *Are both perhaps present in time future,*
> *And time future contained in time past.*
> *If all time is eternally present*
> *All time is unredeemable.*
> *What might have been is an abstraction*
> *Remaining a perpetual possibility*
> *Only in a world of speculation.*
> *What might have been and what has been*
> *Point to one end, which is always present.*

Eliot's speculations on time tease us out of thought. If we read the statements of the opening five lines with logical strictness, they suggest the contrived corridors of *Gerontion*. We are locked into the temporal dimension and live in a fixed present absolutely determined by a past which cannot be altered. The future is equally determined; its nature and quality are functions of the present moment which, in terms of the argument, quickly becomes the past. The dilemma is one more of theory than actuality. Eliot considers time in the abstract; he reasons as if the temporal realm were a construct in formal logic or mathematics. But the *Quartets* seek transcendence of time through certain significant events experienced by human consciousness, through moments that are paradoxically "involved with past and future." These moments give time its substance simply because our practical experience of the temporal process is never without the coloration and bulk of events and their physical and psychological particularities. Certain of these events, experienced at moments of intensified consciousness, reach beyond time and affirm the actuality of an eternal realm. From the Christian point of view, eternity stands outside the temporal realm yet is intimate to it. Reinhold Niebuhr remarks, "[Eternity] stands over time in the sense that it is the ultimate source and power of all derived and dependent existence. It is not a separate order of existence . . . The eternal is the ground and source of the temporal."[12]

> *To communicate directly with the eternal,*
> *. . . to apprehend*
> *The point of intersection of the timeless*
> *With time, is an occupation for the saint—*

The saint has direct apprehension of the eternal. God opens up the future for him and reveals the shape of the apocalypse to come; or God captures her soul in an act of divine sexual violence. But few of us experience the visions of John on Patmos or the raptures of a Saint Teresa; what we are vouchsafed, Eliot tells us,

> *. . . is only the unattended*
> *Moment, the moment in and out of time,*
> *The distraction fit, lost in a shaft of sunlight,*
> *The wild thyme unseen, or the winter lightning*
> *Or the waterfall, or music heard so deeply*
> *That it is not heard at all, but you are the music*
> *While the music lasts.*

None of these moments is outside the experience of "normal" men and women. Through sight, smell ("The wild thyme unseen"), and hearing we break through the closed circle of our ego to grasp the higher reality. For the poet it cannot be otherwise; the *Quartets* explore every familiar aspect of the temporal dimension: the rhythms of cosmic movement, the cyclical return of the seasons, and the more delicately regulated rhythms of biological process. Each of these experiences holds a potential for transcendence; that is, the experience in time is overshadowed by intimations of God's presence.

The experience of "music heard so deeply/That it is not

heard at all" brings human consciousness closest to the heart of time's mystery. When we are listening deeply to a musical work (not dreaming to it or using it to channel our distractions), we apprehend that the sounds move from point *then* to point *now,* defining the flow of time. When the playing of the music ceases, the work exists "in memory only"; both the *then* and *now* are in the past, "Remaining a perpetual possibility." Because music has little status as an object (a palpable *thing* in space) but extraordinary powers as a remembered structure of feelings, music does ideal metaphoric and analogic work in the *Quartets.* Music, the time-dominated art *par excellence,* conquers time; it reaches into the silence where the boundaries of the temporal are penetrated and opposites are reconciled.

The *Quartets* have often been linked to the last quartets of Beethoven. It is difficult to demonstrate literal resemblances, but we can see certain analogous stylistic and technical procedures. We also encounter in Beethoven and Eliot an affective world markedly similar in gesture, tension, and resolution. We are plunged into a context of ambiguity, surprise, sudden changes in mood, unexpected contradictions, and final affirmation. The most striking analogue is that Beethoven's quartets and Eliot's *Quartets* are cyclical and organic structures. Beethoven's quartets expand from controlling musical ideas. In the Quartet in C# Minor (opus 131), everything grows out of the opening fugue and its seminal motif G#, B#, C#, A. Similarly, in the Quartet in A Minor (opus 132), a four note motif provides a center for the entire musical structure.

Each of Eliot's *Quartets* elaborates a central theme; each radiates out from a proposition on the nature of time, on the meaning of history, on the flow of the great river, and on the paradox of the seasons. Every theme implies its opposite, its musical inversion. Man, alienated from self and society, finds reconciliation in God. Despair becomes a way to hope; time and history become ways leading out of time and beyond history. We stress that Eliot's method is not to turn conceptual language into merely pleasing sound and create verbal music through the use of insistent meters and obvious sound effects. The musicality of the *Quartets* inheres in the development of propositional sense and in the application of certain musical techniques to syntax, thematic imagery, metrics, and the large structures of movements and poems. We encounter such specific music procedures as rhythmic expansion and diminution, the transformation of thematic material, and the inversion of themes. Eliot's proposition forming the opening line of "East Coker,"

In my beginning is my end . . .

is reversed at the end of the poem,

In my end is my beginning.

This kind of manipulation is analogous to the inversion of a fugal subject. Other kinds of repetition suggest sonata-form; the first movement of "Burnt Norton" concludes with an exact restatement of lines nine and ten of the opening section:

What might have been and what has been
Point to one end, which is always present.

This returning to the beginning (many times repeated in the *Quartets*) is a structural reenforcement of a cyclical vision of time and the attempt to recapture both a real and an imagined past.

There are many moments of transcendence in the *Quartets* when consciousness reaches a state of exalted detachment and utter involvement; when a moment "in and out of time" gathers sudden coherence. In "Burnt Norton" Eliot leads us

Down the passage which we did not take
Towards the door we never opened
Into the rose-garden . . .

The rose-garden, "our first world," is inhabited by talking birds and roses that

Had the look of flowers that are looked at.

The garden vibrates with "unheard music" and the laughter of unseen children; "an unseen eyebeam" (recalling Donne's "The Extasie") sweeps over the scene. Dominated by these disembodied sense-impressions, the rose-garden develops an ominous atmosphere which is suddenly brightened by an Eastern vision of spiritual unity:

> *And the pool was filled with water out of sunlight,*
> *And the lotos rose, quietly, quietly,*
> *The surface glittered out of the heart of light . . .*

The vision, existing only in imagined time, vanishes. A loquacious bird cautions the wanderer in the garden to go and (rather sententiously) moralizes

> *. . . human kind*
> *Cannot bear very much reality.*

Other exploratory thrusts, moments of blazing epiphany or slow-motion screenings of the historical past, further open the temporal dimension. Eliot's understanding of the temporal process does not always harmonize with the Christian understanding of history as redemptive and linear. (Again, we must emphasize that the *Quartets* are heterodox and even heretical.) We hear a number of chords which, despite Eliot's dialectical skill, remain unresolved. Eliot's excursions into "Eastern Thought" and his bemused fussings "about what Krishna meant" strengthen a notion (for it can only be a notion in Eliot's total context) that time is the veil of Maya, essentially an illusion. If time is not "real," then Christian redemption is impossible; if only through time time is conquered, then time must possess historical substantiality. If time is not "real," then the Incarnation is only a literary symbol and not that moment in time when God becomes man and enters human history.

As a Christian, Eliot would see Christ's presence in history as unbroken and continuous; as the poet of *Four Quartets,* he sees the Incarnation as intermittent, intersecting the linear movement of history. Although the *Quartets* resound with "the sound of the sea bell's perpetual angelus . . ." and other Incarnational music, the Incarnation does not communicate an undimmed vision in which every life and every moment of life gleam with redemptive possibility. Rather, the Incarnation makes dramatic appearances as a fighter plane which is also the Dove of the Annunciation or as a spring day in winter, "not in time's covenant." Perhaps the conflict between the line of history and the periodicity of God's grace is more theoretical than actual, occasioned by the demand that poetry be dramatic and concrete. Incarnation and apocalypse, each of which has specific status in Christian theology, become in *Four Quartets* fictions of imagination which deal in psychological states rather than doctrinal certainties.

Eliot's linking together of beginnings and ends recalls us to the myth of Eternal Recurrence. The pilgrimage to The City of God travels along Heraclitus's road where

> . . . *the way up is the way down, the way forward the
> way back.*

The Christian mythos, which does not encompass a "philosophy of history" but more precisely a theology of history, repudiates all doctrines which assert that man's fate is to experience time past and time future in endless cycles of recurrence. Old Testament and Christian theories of history progress from a definite beginning to a definite goal. For the believing Christian, history moves from Eden to Calvary and then beyond—out of history and to the City of God. Again, Eliot sets aside doctrinal givens for the evidences of experience. In nature and in psychological life, we know that the same things happen again and again. Nature's processes are cyclical; properly speaking, nature has no history but only the ever-returning tides and seasons. It remains the task of *Four Quartets* to reconcile the recurrent time of season and cycle, of biologic process and psychologic *déjà vu*, ". . . a time / Older than the time of chronometers," with man's life in historic time.

Time the container for the thing contained; the thing contained: history. "Burnt Norton," published in 1935, is concerned largely with time and memory; the three succeeding *Quartets,* published during the war years 1940–42, are dense with emblematic event and reflection on the value of historical knowledge. In didactic passages Eliot questions the usefulness of personal experience, the patterns imposed by the conscious recognition of the past, and the putative wisdom of old men. Playing his role of agèd eagle, he asks (in "East Coker"),

> *Had they deceived us,*
> *Or deceived themselves, the quiet-voiced elders,*
> *Bequeathing us merely a receipt for deceit?*
> *The serenity only a deliberate hebetude,*
> *The wisdom only the knowledge of dead secrets*
> *Useless in the darkness into which they peered*
> *Or from which they turned their eyes. There is,*
> *   it seems to us,*
> *At best, only a limited value*
> *In the knowledge derived from experience.*
> *The knowledge imposes a pattern, and falsifies,*
> *For the pattern is new in every moment*
> *And every moment is a new and shocking*
> *Valuation of all we have been.*

The tone is subdued and qualified; there is no Nietzschean polemical zeal to demolish the work of history. Limiting phrases (vocalized pauses), ". . . it seems to us/At best, only . . ." and the remote editorial *we* place Eliot at some distance from his cautious epistemological skepticism.

These exploratory questions, confined at first to the history of the single human being imprisoned in his own experience, gather momentum in succeeding passages. The questions of pattern and meaning make thematic appearances in "The Dry Salvages":

> *It seems, as one becomes older,*
> *That the past has another pattern, and ceases to*
> *   be a mere sequence—*
> *Or even development: the latter a partial fallacy*
> *Encouraged by superficial notions of evolution,*
> *Which becomes, in the popular mind, a means of*
> *   disowning the past.*

A man's personal life is linked to the lives of others and its meaning becomes a matter

> *. . . of many generations—not forgetting*
> *Something that is probably quite ineffable:*

> *The backward look behind the assurance*
> *Of recorded history, the backward half-look*
> *Over the shoulder, towards the primitive terror.*

The last two lines echo a fiercer orchestration of a similar assertion in *The Waste Land:*

> *But at my back in a cold blast I hear*
> *The rattle of the bones, and chuckle spread from*
>   *ear to ear.*

The primitive terror is muted in *Four Quartets;* it can be heard, however, in the untamed ocean,

> *Through the dark cold and the empty desolation,*
> *The wave cry, the wind cry, the vast waters*
> *Of the petrel and the porpoise.*

and in the flow of the great river,

>   *. . . ever, however, implacable,*
> *Keeping his seasons and rages, destroyer, reminder*
> *Of what men choose to forget.*

The meaning passes from the life of man to his origins in nature. Historical knowledge is changed in the remembering: distorted by guilt and dimmed by conscious and unconscious impulses to forget. In nature, in the sea and the river, the rhythm is eternal, recurring and immutable. Eliot's nature is subdued—although there are moments in "Little Gidding" when

> *The brief sun flames the ice, on pond and ditches,*
> *In windless cold that is the heart's heat . . .*

This is the sacramental vision blazing forth the immanence of the Holy Spirit. But more often nature is the "strong brown god"

> *Keeping his seasons and rages, destroyer, reminder*
> *Of what men choose to forget.*

The river serves to warn men of their limitations and their helplessness before the cycle of endless change and recurrence which is the law of nature.

"Little Gidding," the last *Quartet,* brings us to the "recurrent ending of the unending": a fiery apocalypse in the bombed streets of wartime London. The moment of the great fire raids on London is a type for the suspension of historical process; it is equally a "recurrent ending," a moment within historical process and understood as one of many such repeated moments of hypothetical ending. Eliot, as prophet, knows and does not know the meaning of the end. Such knowledge inspires anxiety; Eliot again speculates about the backward devils. In "The Dry Salvages" he catalogues the ways of false prophecy:

> *To communicate with Mars, converse with spirits,*
> *To report the behaviour of the sea monster,*
> *Describe the horoscope, haruspicate or scry . . .*
> > *all these are*
> *usual*
> *Pastimes and drugs, and features of the press . . .*

False prophets predict, through earthquake, fire, or the imminence of revolutionary violence, the catastrophic end to history. Their predictions are "disconfirmed" and the world continues.

Eliot knows, then, that the ending is always recurrent; that the apocalypse we think we have experienced is never the actual Second Coming but only a moment of crisis. No moment of crisis is unique but some moments, experienced with particular intensity, may be transfigured "in another pattern." Two crises, one "now and in England," during the Battle of Britain, the other the English Civil War, figure as apocalyptic moments in "Little Gidding." Two contending parties in the Civil War, Charles I ("a king at nightfall") and John Milton ("one who died blind and quiet") are reconciled in the historical process as the process transfigures the passions and struggles of three hundred years ago into higher meanings:

> *These men, and those who opposed them*
> *And those whom they opposed*
> *Accept the constitution of silence*
> *And are folded in a single party.*
> *Whatever we inherit from the fortunate*

> *We have taken from the defeated*
> *What they had to leave us—a symbol:*
> *A symbol perfected in death.*

Significant historical knowledge is not the recital of past misery and factional bitterness. It is mediation between what we think the past to be, given "with such supple confusions," and true history revealed "in a pattern of timeless moments." The way of ignorant alienation from historical knowledge must be repudiated:

> *A people without history*
> *Is not redeemed from time, for history is a pattern*
> *Of timeless moments. . . .*

But the way of insight, vouchsafed through personal suffering and apocalyptic revelation, brings Eliot to the chapel at Little Gidding and the end of his exploration of time and history:

> *So, while the light fails*
> *On a winter's afternoon, in a secluded chapel*
> *History is now and England.*

From *Gerontion* to *Four Quartets* Eliot tells us that historical knowledge begins in man's unstable memory and his uncertainty about the meaning of events. If our minds are sufficiently instructed and our souls properly humbled, we can trust history to guide us in action. *Gerontion* allows us to see historical process as energy, which like electricity is known by its effects. *Four Quartets* confirms Eliot's first intuitions about the questionable shape of historical knowledge and brings the Christian myth to function as a prime metahistorical fiction. *Gerontion* hesitates between process and knowledge, between the surge of revolutionary force which is modern history and the paralyzing awareness that men are helpless before this force. The process overwhelms knowledge; indeed, makes knowledge (as Nietzsche foretold) a deterrent to action. *Four Quartets* attempts to bring knowledge and process into an essential harmony. Not that men are any the less helpless before History; not that the *saeculum,* the historical process as given to human understanding, shows more than the rise and fall of civilizations, and the successive kindling and extinguishing of human hope. But in the light of Eliot's faith, knowledge and process reveal God's plan working its will through time. The *Quartets* leave the suburbs of Hell where the wicked walk in circles; the meaning of history is no longer given in the Unreal Cities but in the City of God.

Eliot is a moderate and at times diffident prophet. Gerontion and Tiresias are anything but heroic figures; Eliot's later avatars—agèd eagle or calm voice of meditation—seem haunted by memories of the backward devils. Irresponsible speculation about the future "clings to the temporal dimension . . ." and is largely the occupation of the bored, the perplexed, and the fraudulent. Of course, the poet as prophet does not gaze into crystal balls; he responds to historical movement and to the agony of his own feelings of rage and impotence, hope and despair. As a Christian Eliot looks ahead to the end of history:

> *When the tongues of flame are in-folded*
> *Into the crowned knot of fire*
> *And the fire and the rose are one.*

This is the meaning that is *never now but always to come;* such knowledge serves to redeem the chaos and horror of the present dismal epoch. As a being immersed in nature and in the ongoing realities of immediate events, Eliot knows there is no escape from time or avoidance of history. He never revokes the historical category or denies that men are part of historical process; and despite Philip Rahv, Eliot does not "conduct a campaign against history precisely in the name of history. . . ."[13] True, Eliot rejects that aspect of historicism which confuses God with History and sees salvation in the process itself. Eliot does not identify History with Justice; he knows that men have been both instructed and betrayed by history:

> *History may be servitude,*
> *History may be freedom.*

As a prophet Eliot makes a host of necessary moral distinctions about what history is, what it means, and how we may act in its name. We may reject his attitude of profound secular disillusion and his doctrine of moderate Christian comfort; we cannot ignore his distinctions. They have been reached by no "concitation/Of the backward devils." They have been reached through the prophet's suffering and expressed in the prophet's tongue. His final understanding of history is the understanding of Isaiah, "Have ye not known? have ye not heard? hath it not been told to you from the beginning? have ye not understood from the foundations of the earth?"

IV

W. B. Yeats

Nay, even monsters, though they be unusual and diverse, and some have fallen out but once, yet as they are generally wonders and miracles, they are both past and to come: nor is it news to see a monster under the sun.

—St. Augustine, *The City of God,* XI, xiii.

The universe, which is the same for all, has not been made by any god or man, but it always has been, is, and will be— an ever-living fire, kindling itself by regular measures and going out by regular measures.

—Heraclitus, *Fr. 29* (Wheelwright).

I

Prophecy, we have noted, is an expression of heightened historical consciousness. By "historical consciousness" I do not mean the writer's awareness of tradition and chronicle but his awareness of living in the stream of events and the turbulent currents which *are* history. The writer as prophet responds to the dynamism and supposed direction of historical process. Henry Adams, broken by the new energies he cannot comprehend, invokes a divinity whose existence he denies and whose efficacy reaches only his feelings. Eliot sits in the midst of the European dissolution, knowing that time is running out but pleading that all may not be lost; it is not yet the moment to cry *sauve qui peut* but to *think:*

> *Think at last*
> *We have not reached conclusion, when I*
> *Stiffen in a rented house . . .*

"Think at last . . ." It is very late and perhaps the end is near; this may be your last thought but think, damn you, think. Something may yet come from thought, even from a dry brain in a dry season. Tiresias also looks toward the end, a disembodied consciousness recording the apparent simultaneity of all experience, past and present. He sees "the decay of Eastern Europe," the hooded hordes of a millennial revolt, and a hallucinated vision of falling towers.

Yeats as a prophetic poet escapes historical pessimism. He too believes that the end is in view, or that perhaps it has already come. Such knowledge, far from being beyond forgiveness, can occasion great rejoicing. Yeats's vision of the end presages neither man's extinction nor his salvation *supra orbem et in paradiso;* it is one phase of a vast cycle which cannot but choose to pursue a course of perpetual renewal. That an age appears to be concluding, that violence erupts and blood is smeared on the sacred images, are signs of imminent rebirth. At a critical moment, when the energies of the old epoch are exhausted, a new force appears and the historical wheel turns in the opposite direction.

Yeats's theory of history, outlined in *A Vision* and embodied in his prophetic lyrics, derives from the myth of Eternal Recurrence. Yeats was reading Nietzsche in 1902. Nietzsche's name and doctrine figure in *A Vision;* he is the man of Phase Twelve, "called the Forerunner because fragmentary and violent"; he is also the prophet of a new European transformation who "yet . . . when the doctrine of the Eternal Recurrence drifts before his eyes, knows for an instant that nothing can be so transformed . . . ."[1]

Nietzsche's myth of recurrence grew out of the necessity to forge a doctrine transcending impossible alternatives. After proclaiming the death of God and the consequent meaninglessness of salvation through faith, man is condemned to live "alone, in a radically desacralized and immanent world . . . the world of history."[2] But Nietzsche also rejected the Hegelian hope that man will be redeemed through the reconciling process of the historical spirit: in concrete terms, through political and social renovation. Without God and without the Hegelian God-Who-Is-History, Nietzsche relocates human destiny in a transcendent present in which "the world is finished in every single moment and its end attained."[3]

We can read Nietzsche's recurrence as a doctrine for cheering oneself up, an almost Emersonian mode of self-therapy. (Nietzsche greatly admired Emerson.) Men should live *now* and not in History, men should live *as if* every act will be eternally repeated. Men should joyously assent to this destiny because human status is enhanced if they can courageously admit their bondage on the wheel of recurrence. The doctrine crumbles if we seek confirmation of it in physical laws; and although Nietzsche (as well as Yeats) was affected by pre-Socratic and Stoic ideas of world cycles, the recurrence was not formulated as a verifiable theory of history. The Eternal Recurrence discovers in change itself, in the shifting and inconclusive nature of existence, a principle of stability and protection *from* history. If man meets himself eternally, if his actions repeat only what has been previously acted, he can be neither surprised nor disappointed. His will is strengthened because the past is no longer a burden, the future no longer a threat. According to Nietzsche, belief in the providential significance of social and political events corrupts consciousness and enfeebles the will. Men are then powerless before the outrages of History—whether we name History the will of God, the Absolute Spirit developing in time, or the Dialectic of social revolution. The myth of recurrence allows Nietzsche to comprehend the scheme of existence as an eternal Now when time is always redeemed, when (to quote Yeats's "The Gyres"):

> . . . *all things run*
> *On that unfashionable gyre again.*

Yeats never believed in Christian redemptive history. Those pious ax-grinders who would enlist Yeats among the orthodox choose to overlook the irony and blasphemy in his use of Christian symbols. Nor did Yeats find in the political doctrines which were burgeoning in Ireland and Europe any secular eschatology. His experience in practical politics did nothing to build a faith in the liberal concept of history as the progressive betterment of the human condition. A life tangled in the Irish revolutionary movement hardly convinced him that history was a record of noble deeds; it was more nearly an account of complex treachery and mindless violence. Yeats's knowledge led to no vision of history as the tribunal of world-justice. His development of the myth of recurrence provides (as it does for Nietzsche) a center of permanence in the universal flux; and because Yeats was an artist who "withered into truth," the myth became not so much a philosophy against history but a dominant metaphor expressing the form and pressure of modern experience. The myth of recurrence was not a retreat from reality but a powerful mode for its interpretation.

If we ponder the fanciful or quirky parts of *A Vision*, we may wonder what part of "reality" Yeats's cones and gyres, phases and tinctures interpret. If we examine Books IV and V, in which Yeats outlines a scheme of history, we may complain that the scheme scarcely "fits the facts"—despite Yeats's attempt to adjust his system to actual events and confirm his findings in the mingled authority of Hegel, Vico, Henry Adams, Spengler, and many others. But history conceived as the unsorted facts of the past is not reality; historical meaning never resides in events themselves or in the documents recording them. The meaning of history and its radical reality emerge with the application of rational discipline or paradigmatic assumption. (I would argue that Yeats's myth has an inner "logic" no farther from rationality than Hegel's Dialectic; and its paradigm of assumptions will be conjugated in the pages which follows.)

Discipline and assumption must, of course, operate through the power of imagination. Poetic reality is a construct of imagination and not a sum of the empirical data encrusting existence. Yeats's "clear comprehension of the whole" often preceded actual events; not because he possessed occult knowledge (he believed he did) but because his imagination responded to the shocks which agitated the crust of an entire civilization. The poems that speak to the agony of past events are not less "prophetic" than those (like "The Magi" and "The Second Coming") which look ahead to the unspeakable. To grasp Yeats as a poet with holy access to reality does not require mastery of his complex, ironic, and probably spurious system; it only requires that we read his poems and respond to what we already know: our own feelings about the world in which we live.

2

The prophetic poems do not form a special group in Yeats's *Collected Poems*. Nor do I read the *Collected Poems* as a sacred text, a single prophecy whose meaning will yield to the proper interpretation. (Hazard Adams rightly notes that the *Collected Poems* is "a deliberately constructed book"[4]; Yeats worked and reworked individual poems and paid the closest attention to their position and sequence.) It is difficult to name the exact qualities which make a particular poem "prophetic." Many of Yeats's poems are prophetic in tone and mood; they make oracular statements, predict vague disasters, contemplate or exalt violence. Others unfold a controlling idea of historical process. It is these that we shall consider. I make no new discoveries; and the poems I examine have been more fully explicated by other critics. What I hope to show is how the myth of Eternal Recurrence achieves startling relevance: not as a philosophical or cultural doctrine; not as a "solution" (as it seemed to Nietzsche) to the dilemma of the world without God and hence without ethics; but as metaphor and *Weltanschauung*. As a poet's rhythm gives us the ground of his feelings so his basic metaphors open up his view of the world.

"The Magi" (1914) is a poem of Yeats's mature manner in which "the doctrine of the Eternal Recurrence drifts before our eyes. . . ."

> *Now as at all times I can see in the mind's eye,*
> *In their stiff, painted clothes, the pale unsatisfied ones*
> *Appear and disappear in the blue depth of the sky*
> *With all their ancient faces like rain-beaten stones,*
> *And all their helms of silver hovering side by side,*
> *And all their eyes still fixed, hoping to find once more*
> *Being by Calvary's turbulence unsatisfied,*
> *The uncontrollable mystery on the bestial floor.*

These lines (modified iambic hexameter) beat a rhythm of irregular incantation enforcing the harsh energy of the Magi's quest. The Magi were powerful kings who journeyed to witness the birth of a new supernatural order; in Yeats's poem they appear seeking a new dispensation and a new intervention of divinity into the human. The revelation they seek, another incarnation, is strongly intimated in the juxtaposition of quasi-theological abstraction ("uncontrollable mystery") and concrete image ("the bestial floor"). "Bestial floor" evokes erotic violence; and in a later poem, "Leda and the Swan," Yeats celebrates his version of incarnation as a god in animal form coupling with a girl. "Uncontrollable mystery" also suggests the fated, inexorable, and overwhelming reappearance of the Dionysian element in historic life: the periodic return of regressive myth which subverts the rational elements in human consciousness and social reality.

The Magi not only look for the return of the irrational, but in a sinister way ("Being by Calvary's turbulence unsatisfied") profoundly desire it. They are "the pale unsatisfied ones" and the source of their dissatisfaction may be glimpsed in an earlier poem of apocalyptic yearning and ninety-ish world weariness, "The Valley of the Black Pig":

> *The dews drop slowly and dreams gather: unknown spears*
> *Suddenly hurtle before my dream-awakened eyes,*
> *And then the clash of fallen horsemen and the cries*
> *Of unknown perishing armies beat about my ears.*
> *We who will labour by the cromlech on the shore,*
> *The grey cairn on the hill, when day sinks drowned in dew,*
> *Being weary of the world's empires, bow down to you,*
> *Master of the still stars and of the flaming door.*

The poet longs for violence as he dreams in the twilight; he is "weary of the world's empires" and filled with the awareness that his century (the poem was published in 1899) is drawing to a close. This is wanly passionate music for the end of time. Written in the same meter and stanza, "The Magi" also seeks the irrational—not in a *fin-de-siècle* dream of imaginary armies but in a hardened vision of a new beginning. Yeats clearly sees the cyclical nature of the Magi's quest without yet recognizing that the irrational is the source of human creative energy; the dark side of being (in "The Gyres": "any rich dark nothing . . .") which is the source and power for historical renewal.

More forceful in prophetic power and more sinewy in

rhythm is the celebrated "The Second Coming." The poem is animated by machinery from *A Vision:* chiefly the image of the gyre and the concept of *Spiritus Mundi* or racial memory. But Yeats had lived through the Easter 1916 Uprising and the Black-and-Tan terrors; the poem takes impetus from Yeats's emotional involvement with the agonies of his country. There is, of course, no reference in the poem to actual events; but as in *Gerontion* we encounter a conceptual center which proposes, in an impassioned didactic tone, a political attitude:

> *Mere anarchy is loosed upon the world,*
> *The blood-dimmed tide is loosed, and everywhere*
> *The ceremony of innocence is drowned;*
> *The best lack all conviction, while the worst*
> *Are full of passionate intensity.*

This passage appears between the image of bird and gyre and the concluding section, *crescendo e fortissimo,* which unfolds the deliberate progress of the rough beast. It has often been cited as Yeats's comment on the activities of certain public men; Yeats may have had specific men in mind for *The best* and *the worst.* But the strength of the lines lies in their openness of reference. Every generation can discover suitable candidates among the weak, the foolish, the corrupt, and the demonically evil to fill the roles of *best* and *worst.*

"The Second Coming" has been adduced as Yeats's intuitive recognition of the rise of totalitarian rule. In letters to Ethel Mannin and Ernst Toller, Yeats (in nearly identical language) claimed the poem ". . . written some sixteen or seventeen years ago . . . foretold what is happening. I have written of the same thing again and again . . . I am not callous, every nerve trembles with horror at what is happening in Europe 'the ceremony of innocence is drowned.' " It is not cause for much surprise that Yeats's antennae were tuned to rising tendencies. The emotions of 1916-1922 generated images and moral stances entirely appropriate to Hitlerism and Stalinism; Conor Cruise O'Brien points out: ". . . the Black and Tans were in fact an early manifestation of an outlook and methods which the Nazis were later to perfect."[5] Yeats had sensed the form of history: mob rule, unchecked violence, the impotence of the ethical will, the destruction of legitimate authority and inherited values. These are the enormities Yeats compresses in twenty-two lines, a glimpse into the nature of modern political and cultural reality.

Yeats, we reiterate, is no Christian theorist of historical process. The Eternal Recurrence is a species of heresy; Augustine castigates "the wicked who walk in a circuit: not because their life (as they think) is to run circularly, but because their false doctrine runs round in a circular maze."[6] Yeats's poems on the recurrence dramatize familiar Christian images and marshal an order of ideas which can only appear as blasphemous to orthodox believers. The birth of the rough beast and of Christ are analogous events; the dominant irony that the Coming of the Beast is like the Coming of the Savior. But the pitiless monster of history neither announces nor enforces any ethical message. Christianity brought a new ethical idea; the rough beast brings the disintegration of every established ethical ideal.

Yeats's vision of the first Christian dispensation evokes the awe and fear with which the ancient world responded to this half-Asiatic religion. Yeats announces

> *That twenty centuries of stony sleep*
> *Were vexed to nightmare by a rocking cradle . . .*

One Great Year came to its destined end; another year was given its momentum "by a rocking cradle," the new spiritual force of Christianity. As the twentieth century moment on the wheel of recurrence turns toward the Third Millennium, Yeats tells us that we can expect a new source of historical energy given *its* momentum by violent and terrible forces. "The Second Coming" concludes on the edge of darkness with a self-answering, almost superfluous question, and a rhythmic crux:

> *And what rough beast, its hour come round at last,*
> *Slouches towards Bethlehem to be born?*

If the beast moves toward the holy city, its birth is already accomplished. We know its sphinxlike form, its menacing approach. The unscannable last line poises the entire poem on an unresolved metrical dissonance and an unfulfilled expectation. A powerful forward motion hurtles the poem toward some clearly shaped cadence, some satisfactory channeling or dissipation of energy. But the poet as prophet, like "The lord whose oracle is at Delphi neither speaks nor conceals, but gives signs."[7]

Yeats's mystery play, *The Resurrection,* sets forth a complete paradigm of the recurrence. A Hebrew, a Greek, and a Syrian, followers of the new prophet Jesus, discuss in ways typical of their own religious outlook the nature of His being. To the Hebrew Christ is a paragon of conduct, purely human and utterly compassionate. To the Greek Christ is a phantom without muscle or bone; any other belief is barbaric and unworthy of human knowledge and rationality. To the Syrian, a man of the mysteries who speaks for Yeats, Christ's resurrection appears as the fated return of the irrational. He has read *A Vision:*

> . . . What if there is something that lies outside knowledge, outside order? What if at the moment when knowledge and order seem complete that something appears? . . .
> What if the irrational return? What if the circle begin again?

When the risen Christ appears among them, the Greek touches His beating heart and prophesizes the end of the ancient world:

> O Athens, Alexandria, Rome, something has come to destroy you. The heart of a phantom is beating. Man has begun to die. Your words are clear at last, O Heraclitus. God and man die each other's life, live each other's death.

Yeats was deeply impressed by Heraclitus's aphorism which reads (in Philip Wheelwright's translation): "Immortals become mortals, mortals become immortals; they live in each other's death and die in each other's life."[8] In *A Vision* Yeats names the primary gyres Concord and Discord; they fit into each other and as one diminishes the other increases: "Here the thought of Heraclitus dominates all: 'Dying each other's life, living each other's death.' "[9] Heraclitus's thought not only dominates the solid geometry of Yeats' magical and astrological system; it is also made to characterize Yeats's concept of dynamic, recurrent, and violent incarnation. (That Yeats probably misconstrues Heraclitus hardly matters; he is in good company.) It is incarnation, in Yeats's special understanding of that metaphysical event, which supplies the energizing principle of the recurrence. Essentially it is an interchange of energy; of gods dying to bring life to men; of men dying to reactivate the dead gods. Consider the argument as it informs the two songs introducing and concluding *The Resurrection:*

I

I saw a staring virgin stand
Where holy Dionysus died,
And tear the heart out of his side,
And lay the heart upon her hand
And bear that beating heart away;
And then did all the Muses sing
Of Magnus Annus at the spring,
As though God's death were but a play.

Another Troy must rise and set,
Another lineage feed the crow,
Another Argo's painted prow
Drive to a flashier bauble yet.
The Roman Empire stood appalled:
It dropped the reigns of peace and war
When that fierce virgin and her Star
Out of the fabulous darkness called.

II

In pity for man's darkening thought
He walked that room and issued thence
In Galilean turbulence;
The Babylonian starlight brought
A fabulous, formless darkness in;
Odour of blood when Christ was slain
Made all Platonic tolerance vain
And vain all Doric discipline.

Everything that man esteems
Endures a moment or a day.
Love's pleasure drives his love away,
The painter's brush consumes his dreams;
The herald's cry, the soldier's tread
Exhaust his glory and his might:
Whatever flames upon the night
Man's own resinous heart has fed.

These lines begin in a fireworks of mythical allusion; proceed through the deaths of Dionysus and his successor in the cycle, Christ, and end in the wholly human pathos of mutability and exhausted power. Dionysus (as Nietzsche characterized him) is lord of the recurrence; Christ succeeds "In Galilean turbulence" (recalling "Calvary's turbulence" in "The Magi") and brings in a new disorder negating Greek liberality and rationality. Like the rocking cradle and the coming of the rough beast, the violent deaths and miraculous resurrections of the two slain gods are conceived as analogous events. The bloody sacrifice of Dionysus initiates the cycle of the Great Year; the crucifixion and resurrection of Christ initiate the age which saw the destruction of the Roman Empire. Yeats merges the two gods. In the play the frenzied worshippers of Dionysus chant, "God has arisen! God has arisen!" At the same time the resurrected Christ, with warm blood and the beating heart of a living man, walks past the once skeptical but now hysterical Greek into the midst of the apostles.

Dionysus dies into the life of the resurrected man-god Christ; the living Christ becomes the deity and energizing principle of a new historical dispensation. Christ, in turn, dies so that man can live eternally and achieve god-like immortality. Like Eliot's "Christ the tiger," Yeats's Dionysus Christ appears against a background supplied by *The Golden Bough;* the Dionysian mysteries in *The Resurrection* derive from Frazer's descriptions of the orgiastic rites of Adonis and Attis. These rites, commemorating the annual resurrection of the gods, were celebrated throughout the ancient world at the time of the vernal equinox. Yeats locates the rebirth of Christ and Dionysian mysteries in *The Resurrection* derive from Frazer's signs of Pisces and Aries. "Christ rose from the dead at a full moon in the first month of the year, the month that we have named from Mars the ruler of the first [Aries] of the twelve signs."[10] Thus Yeats's Christ also becomes a culture hero emerging from the jungles of comparative religion:

> In the juvescence of the year
> Came Christ the tiger . . .

The new historical dispensation comes from the east.

When western civilization exhausts itself through Caesarism and politics, ". . . the *antithetical* East will beget upon the *primary* West and the child or era so born will be *antithetical*."[11] (*Antithetical* and *primary* are polar terms in Yeats' historico-magical dialectic and may be applied to persons, qualities, night and day, light and dark, abstract thought or concrete phenomena.) Yeats's antithetical East, like Hermann Hesse's ideal of the Karamazov, brings a new influx of historical energy to a declining West. But this energy is not occult power, astrological destiny, or lunar emanation; Yeats drops his mythical mask and explains, "The East, in my symbolism, whether in the circle of the *Principles* or the *Faculties,* is always human power, whether *Will* or *Spirit,* stretched to its utmost."[12] He pursues the reality principle even further and cautiously qualifies the predictive abilities of his system:

> My instructors certainly expect neither a "primitive state" nor a return to barbarism as primitivism and barbarism are ordinarily understood; *antithetical* revelation is an intellectual influx neither from beyond mankind nor born of a virgin, but begotten from our own spirit and history.[13]

Human power and human will, then, impel the historical gyres. Do we assume then that the determinate nature of the system is denied, that sublunary existence moves uninfluenced by *tincture* and *phase,* and that men act as free agents? At the very end of *A Vision* Yeats adds, almost perfunctorily, that human freedom is built into the system; it interacts with necessity in the total dialectic of forces.[14] History is not, however, a record of free human action; the Dionysian will-to-power erupts from the concealed necessity of instinct. Social and political imperatives limit human freedom but so do the darker reasons of the heart. In *The Resurrection* the eviscerated heart of Dionysus beats the rhythm of recurrence; his divinity establishes a new Great Year. But Yeats deliberately modulates his meanings; the miraculous heart of Dionysus beats in the human breast of Christ the man; and in the final lines of the concluding song, we learn that

> *Whatever flames upon the night*
> *Man's own resinous heart has fed.*

This hardly places Yeats in the humanist camp; it does acknowledge, however ambiguously, that the players in the historical drama are not only violent virgins and singing muses. The divine mysteries glow in the light of man's resinous heart; history, conceived as the unending cycle of death and rebirth, has its origin in a wasteful human economy which endlessly consumes its own spiritual substance. Love turns to satiation, creativity to emptiness, action to exhaustion. When the supply of human force runs out, a new interchange of power, another incarnation revives and reverses the historical process. This returns us to the heart of Mystery and the excited words of the Syrian, ". . . there is something that lies outside knowledge, outside order. . . ."

As Yeats' poetry moved steadily "Into the desolation of reality . . ." the intricate symbolism of astrological destiny and slain gods clarified into a mythic simplicity close to Freud's vision of Eros eternally struggling with the destructive power of Thanatos. The power to make and change history resides in the human realm of instinct, primarily in the surging forces of sexuality. That "something outside knowledge, outside order" is libido, *élan vital,* will-to-power: whatever name we wish to apply to that fundamental human energy which is the source both of man's creative transcendence and raging destructiveness. Eros and Thanatos operate at the same dark core of the human process. Freud expressed hope (albeit a qualified one) that at some point in the ongoing crisis of modern history, ". . . eternal Eros will make an effort to assert himself in the struggle with his equally immortal adversary."[15] And as Yeats faced in old age both the termination of his creative existence and civilization on the verge of its greatest war, he dwelt with ferocious clarity on the sexual theme.

3

Yeats must be numbered among the secular apocalyptists insofar as his yearning for the end sought some consummation in a new political order for Europe and Ireland. Secular apocalyptism has a long tradition. Joachim of Flora foretold, in the thirteenth century, the end of history in an imminent Third Age of the Holy Spirit. In that age both secular and eternal realms would co-exist under the leadership of a *novus dux,* a leader combining in the same person both political and spiritual authority. During the Reformation numerous millenarian sects (especially the Anabaptists and the followers of the bloody and insane Jan Bockelson of Münster) proclaimed the Kingdom of God on earth, and in a few spectacular cases actually instigated revolutionary action and experimented with new forms of communal living.[16]

Yeats looked about for a *novus dux,* a charismatic man on horseback who might lead civilization back to a legendary time when the aristocracy practiced the fine arts and the folk made folk art. He was more than an interested spectator to the rise of European fascism, and for a while an excited partisan of the Irish Blue Shirt movement. Its leader General O'Duffy turned out to be no *novus dux;* the movement failed and Yeats, with characteristic prudence, backed off. But if Yeats's advocacies as a man of practical politics showed, at best, misplaced enthusiasm, he harbored impulses which were more than the innocent attraction of a poet toward the fine energies displayed in a good fight. He knew the tragic contradictions of violent action yet he was intrigued by violence. Mob fury and the rule of the worst were symptoms of radical changes in the structure of civilization. It is through violence that history appears to act without ambiguity; violence changes consciousness and transvalues values. A violent world convinced Yeats that the historical process was active and alive:

> *Hurrah for revolution and more cannon shot!*
> *A beggar upon horseback lashes a beggar on foot.*
> *Hurrah for revolution and cannon come again!*
> *The beggars have changed places, but the lash goes on.*
> "THE GREAT DAY"

Violence also provides a nexus between historical process and creative process. As an apocalyptist Yeats urges us to consider not only the cycle of recurrence, but also the holy city of Byzantium where God's holy fire is neither punitive nor redemptive but eternally creative:

> *Flames that no faggot feeds, nor steel has lit,*
> *Nor storm disturbs, flames begotten of flame,*
> *Where blood-begotten spirits come*

> *And all complexities of fury leave,*
> *Dying into a dance,*
> *An agony of trance,*
> *An agony of flame that cannot singe a sleeve.*

Byzantium is Yeats's eternal realm and as such is a metaphor for the creative process. Unlike Eliot's Christian realm of eternity, which reaches *down into* the temporal and completes and justifies historical existence, Yeats's Byzantium is built from below. The fire of Eliot's "Little Gidding" flickers from either hell or purgatory; it is divinely ordained for man's allotted span of purification or eternal torment. Existentially interpreted, Eliot's fire images human suffering and his austere understanding of the grim alternatives life in this world offers. Yeats's fire is also eternal but is not an instrument of God's efficacy in either this world or the next; it resembles Heraclitus's universal substance which ". . . always has been, is, and will be—an ever living fire, kindling itself by regular measures and going out by regular measures."

Byzantium, I have said, is built from below; its miraculous architecture and ghostly forms, transcending "all complexities of mire and blood," depend on those natural and human substances. In the last stanza of "Byzantium," Yeats returns to the mire and blood disdained by images of art and eternity:

> *Astraddle on the dolphin's mire and blood,*
> *Spirit after spirit! The smithies break the flood,*
> *The golden smithies of the Emperor!*
> *Marbles of the dancing floor*
> *Break bitter furies of complexity,*
> *Those images that yet*
> *Fresh images beget,*
> *That dolphin-torn, that gong-tormented sea.*

All the rich and recondite imagery of Byzantium—its cold dancing fire, its changeless metal singing bird, and superhuman forms—issues out of nature's energy, the sexual source of all creative gestures, spiritual reincarnations, and the cycle of recurrence.

"Byzantium" is one of Yeats's full-dress performances in his programmatically grand post-symbolist manner; every image derives from a set context and generates a calculated resonance. More explicit as an expression of the primacy of sexual energy is the late "News for the Delphic Oracle." A climate sweetened by Pan's "intolerable music" blows across a landscape peopled by the mystically-minded Greek philosophers Pythagoras and Plotinus, and representatives of Irish, Christian, and Greek mythology. Oisin and Niamh, Peleus and Thetis, and the Holy Innocents slaughtered by Herod inhabit this very physical heaven whose transcendence is not achieved through the fabrications of art but through that Dionysian fury which is the spur to human creativity. The poem ends with the frank description of a sexual orgy:

> *Foul goat-head, brutal arm appear,*
> *Belly, shoulder, bum,*
> *Flash fishlike; nymphs and satyrs*
> *Copulate in the foam.*

These lines evoke Hegel's sentiment that nothing great happens in human affairs without passion.[17] If we join Freud's insight about Eros and Thanatos to Hegel's sentiment, we have traveled to Yeats's final domain where the power spinning the gyres is generated by the utterly and basically human.

Yeats recorded in "The Second Coming" the birth of the beast. As he watched Europe drive toward the Second World War, he saw the beast develop into a vigorous man-monster. Doubtless he derived bitter satisfaction in seeing his prophecy confirmed; but he also gazed beyond the reign of the beast and the fated destruction of his own epoch. "The Gyres," Yeats' last extended expression of the theory outlined in *A Vision,* begins in near-hysterical exultation at what the terrible changes of history have wrought and ends on a note of defiant optimism:

THE GYRES

> *The gyres! the gyres! Old Rocky Face, look forth;*
> *Things thought too long can be no longer thought,*
> *For beauty dies of beauty, worth of worth,*
> *And ancient lineaments are blotted out.*
> *Irrational streams of blood are staining earth;*
> *Empedocles has thrown all things about;*

Hector is dead and there's a light in Troy;
We that look on but laugh in tragic joy.

What matter though numb nightmare ride on top,
And blood and mire the sensitive body stain?
What matter? Heave no sigh, let no tear drop,
A greater, a more gracious time has gone;
For painted forms or boxes of make-up
In ancient tombs I sighed, but not again;
What matter? Out of cavern comes a voice,
And all it knows is that one word "Rejoice!"

Conduct and work grow coarse, and coarse the soul,
What matter? Those that Rocky Face holds dear,
Lovers of horses and of women, shall,
From marble of a broken sepulchre,
Or dark betwixt the polecat and the owl,
Or any rich, dark nothing disinter
The workman, noble and saint, and all things run
On that unfashionable gyre again.

The poem proceeds on a level of barely controlled frenzy. An obsessive rhetoric—the insistent repetitions and the exhortations to rejoice in destruction and laugh at the process which shatters values and brings civilization to its knees—forces Yeats's passion. Yeats asks himself and his reader to confront the enormities of present history and not regret "a more gracious time." But there is more here than Nietzsche's joyous *amor fati* or a commendable tough-mindedness in the face of the inevitable. Although Yeats claims to be only an onlooker, an agitated witness to the End, he is obviously more than an agonized spectator. He is a pseudo-participant in the action, if only as rhetorician. Yeats is urging History along and the rhetoric has the bite of vindictiveness; the message *I told you so!* The voice of prophecy is strained: as if its burden were proving too much for it.

Two crucial Yeatsian ideas confront us: that the rule of the worst has produced artistic and ethical decline; that the signs of doom are also harbingers of rebirth. It is this rebirth, stimulated by the "Lovers of horses and of women," which issues from the same underground power which opens the wound in the world's side and sheds "Irrational streams of blood." Again we confront the paradox central to Yeats's

theory of history: the irrational force which destroys civilizations is the same creative energy which builds them. At a critical point creative energy turns destructive and cultural unity
disintegrates. At another critical point the gyre reverses and
the once-destructive force becomes creative. Thanatos and Eros
exchange places in an eternal dance of the antinomies.

"The Gyres" reiterates two familiar mythologizings of the
rebirth of human energy; the new power shall flow from

> . . . *marble of a broken sepulchre,*
> *Or dark betwixt the polecat and the owl.*

The first reference is Christian. although Yeats expects a
monster from *Anima Mundi* rather than the return of the
Messiah. For Yeats the Resurrection is a symbol for the
creative will which cannot die. "Or dark between the polecat
and the owl" derives from Yeats's lunar metaphysics. The dark
of the moon is history in a time of animality, when the human
gives way before the owl and bat; when good and evil are
confused and the ethical will becomes impotent. Finally,
Yeats drops his mask and says, without mythical or magical
disguise, that Eros, the nakedly human power of "Lovers of
horses and women . . ." shall call from the grave the creative
energy that will re-animate historical recurrence. Life from
death itself, from "any rich, dark nothing . . ."

4

Yeats's myth of Eternal Recurrence raises the question of what
have been called "anti-historical" theories of history. Cyclical
and naturalist theories repudiate the essentially rectilinear
and teleological process discerned by Christian, Hegelian, and
Marxist philosophers and prophets. Indeed, as westerners
bound to Hegelian-Christian concepts, we hardly recognize a
theory of history as "historical" unless it shows linear movement toward some stated goal: the City of God, the ultimate
realization of the Absolute Idea, or the Classless Society. Nor
do we recognize a theory of history as "historical" unless it in
some way shows the features of a theodicy. The suffering men
endure in history must ultimately be justified by salvation in
an extra-historical realm, by belief in social progress and the
betterment of the human condition, or by hope for a utopian

renovation of the political order. Finally, we are skeptical toward theories of history which ignore specific events and regard the political and social as symptoms and not causes of historical reality and change.

The essential features of Yeats's myth contradict history as linear teleology, as theodicy, and as political action. The Eternal Recurrence moves toward no goal other than the destined destruction of a world-era; out of the destruction of one era issues another era which follows a similar (but not necessarily identical) course. Apocalypse, the interruption of historical process, establishes no permanent end to time and history; for Yeats The Second Coming presages a Third and a Fourth. Apocalypse is a recurrent and not, as in Christian belief, a unique event; to paraphrase Marx, apocalypse is the violence necessarily accompanying the birth of a new historical era. And in applying Marx's obstetrical metaphor to Yeats's vision of history, we note that Yeats made the error that Marx's romantic and bloody-minded disciples have made: to think that violence *is* history, that the anguish of the mother is indistinguishable from the new life. (Marx's dramatic pronouncement, "Violence is the midwife of history," of course encourages confusion. The metaphor makes no sense; a midwife should aid the mother in giving birth as easily as possible, with the least amount of violence. What Marx meant was that a woman's childbirth labor and historical process were both violent occasions. But an *allegoria* of Violence as Midwife is grotesque and incomprehensible.)

The Eternal Recurrence neither harmonizes the evil in the world with human moral aspirations nor vindicates God's dealings with men. Hegel calls the method of *The Philosophy of History*

> . . . a Theodicaea—a justification of the ways of God . . . so that the ill that is found in the World may be comprehended, and the thinking Spirit reconciled with the fact of the existence of evil. Indeed, nowhere is such a harmonizing view more pressingly demanded than in Universal History; and it can be attained only by recognizing the *positive* existence, and in which that negative element is a subordinate and vanquished nullity.[18]

The key word here is *reconciled;* Hegel's vision of universal history mediates between the evil found in the world and man's ever-expanding consciousness. Yeats's system does not recognize progressive human renovation, spiritual purification, or redemptive possibilities. Yeats does not share Hegel's mediating optimism that evil will become "vanquished nullity," that the historical process eliminates as merely contingent or non-essential, negative elements. While Hegel takes a more nearly Christian view of evil—that it is a lessening of the good and hence not "real" but a form of abstract deprivation—Yeats pursues a Manichean line. Good and evil contend as equals; we can see in history the endless recurrence of "good" and "evil" epochs.

The pattern of Yeats's history is not determined by events in the political and social realms. In Eliot's vision of history, social and political action form discernible (if tangled) threads through the labyrinth of a declining civilization. Eliot also sees himself in history: in a community of fellow sufferers and sinners. Salvation is not ordained for the exceptional man but for those men deemed morally worthy of salvation. In Yeats's poetic world there is no salvation *from* history. The exceptional man shakes his fist at revolution and political chaos; he may also "laugh in tragic joy." In Eliot God works, mysteriously but surely, through time and history; His presence is made known through the Incarnation. Yeats uses the Incarnation as metaphor; but where the Christian Eliot conceives Incarnation as the reconciliation of God and man, Yeats's images of incarnation dramatize the subduing of a woman by a masculine god. For Yeats theophany replaces theodicy: that is, incarnation does not mediate between the human and divine but violently signals the dominating presence of an all-too-human God. And this God assumes the role of man's crushing metaphysical opponent:

> *Now his wars on God begin;*
> *At stroke of midnight God shall win.*

Political action and social particularity are for Yeats effects and not the causes of history. This is not to say that Yeats's poetry lacks concrete reality, but that for Yeats reality begins in the forms the mind imposes on experience. The pattern of Yeats's history exists before events occur; and men, as historical agents, do not "make history" but fill in the details of an already existing pattern. Hebrew prophets and Christian (and post-Christian) philosophers saw history as a moral drama; the outcome of events was determined by the good or evil actions of men. In Yeats history moves through the interaction of ethically neutral forces. We discover, of course, in Yeats's poetry "practical judgments of value":

> *The best lack all conviction, while the worst*
> *Are full of passionate intensity.*

But historical process is neither good nor evil: it is antithetical or primary; it is of the *fifteenth phase* or the *twenty-second phase;* it is the Age of the Swan or Dove. These are categories of power; moral splendor for Yeats is the heroism of individuals standing up to the vast and pitiless power of historical process.

What links Yeats's mythic interpretation of history to the reality men experienced during years of actual historical crisis? I do not propose to verify the truth of Yeats's interpretation—it does not fit many historical "facts"—but I hope to suggest the grounds of its powerful imaginative appeal. Yeats's myth of Eternal Recurrence is an aesthetic response to human suffering and moral calamity; actual history, the violent occasions of Easter 1916, prompted this cry:

> *All changed, changed utterly:*
> *A terrible beauty is born.*

The oxymoron (a favorite figure in Yeats) *terrible beauty* captures the paradoxical nature of the experience; the destructive power of history destroys men and institutions, but the power itself, History in its metaphysical grandeur, possesses an intrinsic and indestructible fascination. When Yeats exults in his mood of desperate optimism, as in "The Gyres," he strides to war with the God-Who-Is-History; *amor fati,* the strange device woven into Zarathustra's battle-flag, is also Yeats's motto. The Eternal Recurrence then indeed becomes a doctrine to cheer oneself up and gain the courage to face the "desolation of reality": the final, disillusioning insight that man's thought is his own worst enemy and that culture, achieved through intellectual effort, is destroyed by that very effort. This is the burden of "Meru," a late (1935) and important statement of the unending war between knowledge and life, between the restless, never-ending activity of thought and the always contaminating, always compromising world of action:

> *Civilization is hooped together, brought*
> *Under a rule, under the semblance of peace*
> *By manifold illusion; but man's life is thought,*
> *And he, despite his terror, cannot cease*
> *Ravening through century after century,*
> *Ravening, raging, and uprooting that he may come*
> *Into the desolation of reality:*
> *Egypt and Greece, good-bye, and good-bye, Rome!*
> *Hermits upon Mount Meru or Everest,*
> *Caverned in night under the drifted snow,*
> *Or where that snow and winter's dreadful blast*
> *Beat down upon their naked bodies, know*
> *That day brings round the night, that before dawn*
> *His glory and his monuments are gone.*

Hegel also believed that man's life was thought; the development of human consciousness toward what he named Absolute Spirit defined and justified man's life in history. At the imagined end of history (*imagined* because Hegel never speculated on any apocalyptic conclusion to history), we discover Absolute Knowledge divested, we suppose, of all impurities. But the clear movement of thought is impeded by what thought produces; men transform their ideas into cultural realities and in this process of objectification, they necessarily lose part of themselves. Every act of human creation results in the estrangement of self from that which the self creates; this is the meaning of those final lines from *The Resurrection:*

> *Everything that man esteems*
> *Endures a moment or a day,*
> *Love's pleasure drives his love away,*
> *The painter's brush consumes his dreams;*
> *The herald's cry, the soldier's tread*

Exhaust his glory and his might:
Whatever flames upon the night
Man's own resinous heart has fed.

In "Meru" Yeats echoes Hegel's insight (from *The Phenomenology of Mind*) that "The spiritual condition of self-estrangement exists in the sphere of culture as a fact."[19] Men are driven by the urgency of thought to raven and uproot those illusory institutional arrangements we call civilizations. Yeats leaves us right there: in the "desolation of reality," alienated from every past civilization and the labor of men's work. This is Yeats in a mood of bleak and desperate pessimism.

However, the rhythm of the dialectic continues its relentless motion. The alienated spirit, confronting reality stripped of its veil of culture, must return and reconstruct needed illusions. *All is process* Yeats has told us again and again; if "day brings round the night," then night must herald the day. We have read in "The Gyres" (which stands in dialectical opposition to "Meru") that the black desolation of reality shall

              . . . disinter
The workman, noble and saint, and all things run
On that unfashionable gyre again.

Again Yeats's thought is close to Hegel's. Because the world is never still and the souls of men are never content with any reality, whether desolate or thickly inhabited, the alienated self seeks transformation. In the tormented language of *The Phenomenology of Mind,* Hegel tells us that alienation is itself alienated: ". . . existence consists really in transmuting each determinate element into its opposite; and it is only this estrangement that constitutes the essential nature and preservation of the whole . . . the alienation will be found to alienate itself, and the whole thereby will take all its contents back into the ultimate principle it implies . . ."[20]

The ultimate principle for Yeats is immortal process. From poem to poem he reifies the essential doctrines of recurrence and change. These afford both despair and comfort: despair because our age is *antithetical;* comfort because through certain forms of violence we may be brought back to traditional values and a stable civilization. Yeats's version of traditionalism (which resembles Southern agrarianism or Eliots' Idea of a Christian Society) affirms an aesthetic notion of politics and society—a notion that seems to say that the good society is one in which the arts flourish and poets need not work too hard for their living. Erich Heller puts it more strongly and sees a Nietzschean Yeats who took with utmost seriousness Nietzsche's ". . . central dogma of the new philosophy of art: 'Only as an aesthetic phenomenon is the world forever justified.'"[21]

Certainly the very Nietzschean doctrine of Eternal Recurrence adumbrates a theory of history which turns the world of action and event into an aesthetic structure. *A Vision* is no philosophy of history; it is a poem whose form and theme exist in metaphoric relationships to the historical world. The apocalypse forming the spectacular conclusion to Yeats's vision of historical process has startling relevance to actual history, to what the modern world has suffered through social and political change. This relevance, this prophetic aptness, however deepened by Yeats's awareness of actual history, was as much a matter of aesthetic temperament as it was of experience; Yeats was already dreaming, in the very early (and woefully immature) *The Wanderings of Oisin,*

> *A Druid dream of the end of days*
> *When the stars are to wane and the world be done.*

Yeats took a certain malign satisfaction (as did Henry Adams) in seeing his prophecies of violence being fulfilled. His death occurred on the eve of the Second World War; like Henry Adams, he saw his own impending death congruent with the end of a cataclysmic phase of European history.

Whether Yeats's version of Eternal Recurrence carries us beyond an art for art's sake theory of history or whether it remains a philosophy (or myth) *against* history depends on what we expect poetry (and art generally) to do for us. We certainly cannot expect salvation from history through poetry; Erich Heller, again speaking about Yeats and Nietzsche, tells us ". . . there is no salvation through consciously induced spontaneities, and there is no salvation through Art."[22] That is, Yeats's belief that civilization might be refreshed and reintegrated through periodic explosions of raw creative energy is a desperate and destructive doctrine; that Yeats at times believed such a doctrine seems clear. I quote from "Under Ben Bulben," that final rant concluding *The Collected Poems:*

> *You that Mitchel's prayer have heard,*
> *"Send war in our time, O Lord!"*
> *Know that when all words are said*
> *And a man is fighting mad,*
> *Something drops from eyes long blind,*
> *He completes his partial mind,*
> *For an instant stands at ease,*
> *Laughs aloud, his heart at peace.*
> *Even the wisest man grows tense*
> *With some sort of violence*
> *Before he can accomplish fate,*
> *Know his work or choose his mate.*

We can dismiss this as the death-bed bluster of a typical "pseudo man-of-action," of one whose awareness of the suffering and cruelty of war is obscured by romantic nonsense. Or we can view Yeats's doctrine as Nietzschean in assigning a therapeutic function to violence. Men and societies suffering psychic illness may be healed of their corruption and self-indulgence through the harsh medicine of war.

Neither the romantic nor the therapeutic view of war and violence holds any attractiveness in an age of technological overkill. But some concept of therapy may mediate between history and salvation. Philip Rieff points out that in The Age of Psychological Man the quest for salvation becomes a quest for therapy; the need for psychic healing now holds the power ". . . to bind and loose men in the conduct of their affairs with reasons which sink so deeply into the self that they become commonly and implicitly understood."[23] Norms for conduct and goals defining social achievement—traditionally demanded by men from their culture—are no longer derived from religious belief but from self-conscious awareness of psychic need. No poetry, not even Yeats's best poetry, provides us with salvation from the terrors of history; it may, however, give us the terms for psychologically alleviating that terror.

These terms comprise a therapeutic, what Auden praises in his "In Memory of W. B. Yeats":

For Poetry makes nothing happen: it survives
In the valley of its saying where executives
Would never want to tamper, it flows south
From ranches of isolation and the busy griefs,
Raw towns that we believe and die in; it survives,
A way of happening, a mouth.

We then understand the Eternal Recurrence as Nietzsche understood it: as a psychological bulwark against despair and the intolerable loneliness of living in a world without divine sanctions. The Eternal Recurrence is not a "solution" to the problem of history; like all poetic fictions it gives plausible form to our feelings.

V

The Cantos *of Ezra Pound*

". . . what are all the records of history but narratives of
successive villanies, of treasons and usurpations, massacres
and wars?"

—Samuel Johnson

I

On the jacket of *Section: Rock Drill | 85–95 | de los cantares,*
Pound announces the message of the *Cantos.* He makes no
pretense that they erect a self-sufficient poetic world; he tells
us the *Cantos* are

> . . . the tale of the tribe . . . it is their purpose to give
> the true meaning of history as one man has found it: in
> the annals of ancient China, in the Italian Renaissance,
> in the letters and diaries of Jefferson, the Adamses and
> Van Buren, in the personalities of his own time. The
> lies of history must be exposed; the truth must be ham-
> mered home by reiteration, with the insistence of a rock
> drill.

For those who might wish to read the *Cantos* for their "lyrical"
qualities and ignore Pound's message about history, we have:
"To hell with cookie-pushers who think poetry is a bun shop
and are busy making eclairs." Such statements of purpose,
given with such defensive pugnacity, often exert little more
pressure than the air which is the weight of words. But Pound
is intensely serious; he means us to regard the *Cantos* as a
didactic poem about history. Even more. He exhorts the reader

to consider the *Cantos* as part of history itself. They intend not only to instruct our memories but also to involve us in events; we "become" history as we immerse ourself in Pound's discourse. And after the lies of history have been exposed, after we have absorbed Pound's message, we presumably move to action.

The critic may choose to disregard Pound's statement that the *Cantos* are propaganda about "the true meaning of history." Pound has given many different explanations about the structure and content of his life work; these explanations tend to cancel each other out. On the one hand, we have heard that the *Cantos* are purely spatial in form, depending not on the usual syntactical arrangement of language but on visual juxtapositions, the so-called "truth of ideograms." On the other hand, Pound and a number of his critics have described the *Cantos* as a giant musical composition, an intricate fugue weaving together many diverse thematic strands, or a great "ground bass" (a passacaglia, I suppose) sustaining an enormous set of complex variations. One critic, Hugh Kenner, tells us the *Cantos* are both musical *and* ideogrammatic; this makes Pound a successor to Wagner and the *Cantos* some kind of audiovisual *Gesamtkunstwerk*.[1] Unfortunately, no critic has explained how language can function without syntax in a long poem; while the ideogram may be a useful analogy to describe the methodology of the short imagist poem, it hardly "explains" the structure of a poem which is now seventeen cantos longer than *The Divine Comedy*. Nor do the musical explainers discover anything more than a few repeated phrases and rhythms to bolster the theory that the *Cantos* is another *Art of the Fugue* or *Passacaglia in C Minor*.

However the critics have attempted to dodge the central problem of the *Cantos,* the problem remains. It is not a question of whether the *Cantos* are organized musically or spatially, whether they employ the techniques of the plastic or the musical arts or both. It is whether the *Cantos* fulfill the formal requirements of a long poem. Are they fleshed with a coherent imagery and symbolism, are they boned with a consistent carrying metric? Is Pound's message about history absorbed into metaphor and myth, archetype and ideogram?

Does the poem reach through its identity of form and subject its own version of historical truth? Does the structure of the *Cantos*, its poetic process, offer an imaginative analogue to the historical process? Eliot's Christian eschatology and Yeats's myth of recurrence do not earn universal assent, but Eliot's mediations and Yeats's circularity offer an imaginative grasp of what the historical process *might be*. Hegel has said the world is rational if viewed rationally (a notion of limited value for practical politics or daily encounters). The metaphysical structures of successful poems allow us to glimpse (as if we inhabited Hegel's heaven of Absolute Spirit) a possible rational world.

Despite critical pleading, the *Cantos* are an unfinished, totally flawed, almost totally destroyed poem. The recent volume (1968) of the *Cantos* is called *Drafts & Fragments of Cantos CX-CXVII;* it is not possible to distinguish these clearly labeled notes and drafts from the two earlier volumes *Thrones* and *Section: Rock Drill.* No reader can fail to note the progressive disintegration of substance and surface. The mind loses its way among the scattered bundles of torn documents and fragmentary texts translated (or not translated) from the languages of the world; the ear forgets the vigorous prosodic tune which begins Canto 1 and at the end hears little more than the mutter and buzz of free association. With the best will in the world, the most up-to-date scholarly annotation, and the sharpest exegetical tools, it is impossible to read the macaronic lines which follow and derive pleasure from their music or intellectual stimulation from their propositional sense:

> Coke, Iong Ching,
>   responsabili
> par cretance del ewe which is
>   french for floodwater.
> Who for bridges
>   reparando;
> For every new cottage 4 acres
>   Stat. de 31 Eliz.
>   Angliae amor.
>   Canto 108

If it seems I have selected an uncharacteristic passage, quoted unfairly or out of context, I suggest the reader undertake to parse Cantos 85 through 117.² Little remains of thematic structure, or simple grammatical relationships; we encounter page after page of Kung-fe-tse in the original ideograms, Egyptian hieroglyphics, and misquotations from the classics. In Canto 116 Pound mourns his inability to complete the poem he had once envisioned:

> *a tangle of works unfinished.*
> *I have brought the great ball of crystal;*
> > *who can lift it?*
> *Can you enter the great acorn of light?*
> > *But the beauty is not the madness*
> *Tho' my errors and wrecks lie about me.*
> *And I am not a demigod,*
> *I cannot make it cohere.*

Can criticism make the *Cantos* cohere; can we write the poem Pound, in his own specifically musical sense of the word and by his own admission, failed to *compose?* We find motifs and handfuls of notes; we find vague instructions for scoring. Nowhere do we find a basic tonality or tone-row, a consistent development or climax, a fully orchestrated page. My concern with the *Cantos,* then, centers more on intention and intended method than on intrinsic aesthetic value. The *Cantos* is not an achieved poem, "a window to existence and history," but a shattered mirror crazily reflecting historical knowledge and historical process. I take Pound at his word that he is writing "the tale of the tribe," a poem that means to be exemplary history. There is no reason why histories cannot be framed in verse or told with the grace, precision, and power which poetic form renders human experience. Pound himself discounts the *Cantos* as detached art; and *horrible dictu* and contrary to every canon of post-Symbolist literary theory, stresses their importance as naked propaganda.

Pound faces problems as old as Aristotle. If the *Cantos* is a poem "about" history, if it is a poem containing history, or if (as some critics have affirmed) it *is* history, then we stand deep in an ontological quagmire. A poem *qua* poem is not expected to tell *wie es eigentlich gewesen,* preserve chronology and sequence, or infer patterns of cause and effect. But if the *Cantos* is history told as a poem, then we should expect that it follow the canons governing the writing of humanistic history. If Pound really means to give us knowledge of the past and instruct our wills for right action, then the history of the *Cantos* must separate present and past, sift the true from the false ("the lies of history must be exposed"), and erect a structure of premises, a philosophy or a metaphysic, which shows an inner reality to events as well as their outer factuality. Our interest in the *Cantos* is the same as the controlling interest of this study: what does it say about historical knowledge and historical process? But since we see the *Cantos* as documentary history rather than a finished product of the poetic imagination, we shall examine its specifically historiographical assumptions: does it indeed expose the lies of history, does it clarify the meaning of the past, and does it draw a clear line from past to the present and ". . . affirm the gold thread in the pattern (Canto 116) . . . ."

2

The historical substance of the *Cantos* consists of documentary sources, the matrix out of which history, as the tale of the tribe, is always written. Pound's historical knowledge is communicated in paraphrase, translation, and, in many of the *Cantos,* through direct, copious quotation. Pound describes his use of documents as the method of palimpsest:

> But the record
>   the palimpsest—
> a little light
>   in great darkness—
> cuniculi—
>   Canto 116

The palimpsest by itself is not historical knowledge; it may provide useful information from its many layers of past time but the meaning of a palimpsest depends on its interpretation. Oddly enough, Pound never questions his sources, never seems to doubt that what he put into the *Cantos* is not only historically accurate but utterly relevant to his enterprise. He shows none of the skepticism about knowledge that Nietzsche, Adams, and Eliot show; in his naive American way he assumes the validity of printed matter, of forgotten scandal, and the detritus of personal memory. The attitude of the *Cantos* toward historical knowledge can hardly be described as critical or sophisticated.

I cite the opening passage from Canto 52 to illustrate how Pound apprehends and presents historical material. Canto 52 stands more or less midway in the poem; it looks back toward the first Cantos with their limpidity of versification; it presages the later Cantos with their dissolution of aesthetic surface and mannered unintelligibility.

And I have told you of how things were under Duke
                              Leopold in Siena
   And of the true base of credit, that is
                              the abundance of nature
with the whole folk behind it.
"Goods that are needed" said Schacht (anno seidici)
commerciabili beni, deliverable things that are wanted.
                              neschek is against this, the serpent
And Vivante was there in his paradise, the mild air
   the fields rolling eastward, and the tower half ruin'd
with a peasant complaining that her son was taken for war
and he said "plutocracies were less violent".
                              sin drawing vengeance, poor yitts paying for
paying for a few big jews' vendetta on goyim
I think wrote Miss Bell to her mama
   that when not against the interests of Empire
we shd/ keep our pledges to Arabs.
Thus we lived on through sanctions, through Stalin
   Litvinof, gold brokers made profit
rocked the exchange against gold
Before which entrefaites remarked Johnnie Adams (the elder)
IGNORANCE, sheer ignorance ov the natr ov money
   sheer ignorance of credit and circulation.
Remarked Ben: better keep out the jews
   or yr/ grand children will curse you
jews, real jews, chazims, and neschek
also super-neschek or the international racket . . .

"Under Duke Leopold . . ." was established the Sienese *Monte dei Pasche,* a bank which meets with Pound's approval. [Hjalmar] Schacht was Hitler's minister of finance—one of Pound's fiscal heroes. *Anno seidici* is the year 1937. (The middle Cantos date events by the Italian Fascist calendar which counted 1922, the year Mussolini marched on Rome, as year I.) *Neschek,* "the serpent," is the Hebrew word for usury; it means the bite of a serpent. *Neschek* appears in the text of the Deuteronomic strictures against the taking of interest (Deut. 23:19–20). "Vivante" is Leone Vivante, a friend of Pound and a writer on English poetry. He lived on a hill near Siena, hence "his paradise." "Miss Bell" is Gertrude Lowthian Bell (1868–1926), a celebrated woman traveler in the Near East; she was connected with the British Arab Bureau during World War I and wrote numerous letters and reports on prevailing conditions. "Ben," near the end of the passage, is Benjamin Franklin. Pound quotes from the notorious "Franklin Forgery": the work of anti-Semitic propagandists. Franklin never issued any warning to his fellow colonists about the Jews; his supposed remarks were manufactured in 1934 by an anti-Semitic newspaper.[3] Like *The Protocols of the Elders of Zion,* the "Franklin Forgery" is persistent and unkillable. The appearance of a many-times-exposed forgery in a poem purporting to uncover the lies of history should be duly noted.

The seventeenth century, World War I, the mid-thirties of the twentieth century, and the period of the American Revolution comprise the historical fabric of this passage. It is stitched together with a slender thematic thread, Pound's notions about money and banking. The chronological disorder is deliberate; characters and episodes serve as *exempla:* Duke Leopold (1747–1792) and Hjalmar Schacht (1877–1970) personify such abstractions as "the true base of credit" and "ignorance of credit and circulation." The good guys are Pound's fiscal heroes; the bad guys are bankers and gold brokers. An irritating feature of Pound's method is his continual use of the irrelevant aside; neither Vivante nor Miss Bell figures in the discussion about "the true base of credit." They are both "historical" elements, but it is difficult to see how they bear on the particular argument Pound is pushing.

The simultaneous appearance of Litvinof (1876–1951) and John Adams (1735–1826) of Ben Franklin (1706–1790) arid Duke Leopold in the ongoing present of the *Cantos* typifies the programmatic use of anachronism which is Pound's basic approach to the problem of communicating historical knowledge. Pound, as early as 1910, anticipated the "method" of the *Cantos;* in *The Spirit of Romance* he gives this lyrical account of history:

> It is dawn at Jerusalem while midnight hovers above the Pillars of Hercules. All ages are contemporaneous. It is B.C., let us say, in Morocco. The Middle Ages are in Russia. The future stirs already in the minds of the few. This is especially true of literature, where the real time is independent of the apparent, and where many dead men are our grandchildren's contemporaries, while many of our contemporaries have been already gathered into Abraham's bosom, or some more fitting receptacle.[4]

"All ages are contemporaneous." What is *really* history is what, at the moments of inspiration and composition, serves the poetic enterprise. Events are important in the stimulation they exert on the poet's creative power. Pound's versions of Provence and the Greek Anthology, of Chinese poetry and Propertius hardly raise questions of historical accuracy or justice; they tell no lies for they affirm only the truths of art. If they exploit such anti-historical elements as anachronism and colloquial speech, they do so with an aesthetic end in view:

> *He strove to resuscitate the dead art*
> *Of poetry . . .*

The Pound of the *Personae* did not see himself as a moralist exposing the lies of history but as a craftsman, not as a builder of metaphysical structures but as a writer of songs.

Pound's earlier poetry did not propose a use *for* historical knowledge; it simply made imaginative use *of* it. The *Cantos* propose to retell the history of Western and Chinese culture, and to rescue for the present the achievements of the past. Pound responded to what Nietzsche so bitterly attacked: the nineteenth-century belief in History and its redemptive possibilities. History was meant to function as the major ordering structure in the *Cantos;* historical knowledge could supply a system of belief. As Dante knew his reader believed in God, Pound knew his reader believed that in History truth is revealed and salvation achieved. Far from thinking History a burden, a deterrent to action, Pound believed historical knowledge would energize men to action. Pound remarks, "I am writing to resist the view that Europe and civilization is going to Hell."

The ideogrammatic or anachronistic method (they are identical) would make all of the past instantly present and hence available not only to the imagination but to the will. But the method, as Pound employs it, more nearly prevents than aids historical knowledge, more often confuses than enlightens the reader about the true nature of history.

> *and usury @ 60   or lending*
>   *that which is made out of nothing*
> *and the state* can *lend money   as was done*
> *by Athens for the building of the Salamis fleet*
>   *and if the packet gets lost in transit*
>   *ask Churchill's backers*
>   *where it has got to   the state need not borrow*
>   *nor do the veterans need state guarantees*
>   *for private usurious lending*
>   *in fact that is the cat in the woodshed*
>   *the state need not borrow*
>   *as was shown by the mayor of Wörgl*
>   *who had a milk route*
>   *and whose wife sold shirts and short breeches*
> *and on whose book-shelf was the Life of Henry Ford*
> *and also a copy of Divina Commedia . . .*
>   Canto 74

Three historical instances are present here: the Battle of Salamis (480 B.C.); Churchill's fiscal policies (1940–1945); the credit and borrowing strategy of a certain mayor of a small Austrian town (sometime in the twentieth century?). We know that Pound despises Churchill, that he prefers the Athenians to the Persians, and that the mayor of Wörgl somehow frightened or confused the uppity bankers of Innsbruck:

>   *. . . and when a note of the*
>   *small town of Wörgl went over*

>   *a counter in Innsbruck*
>   *and the banker saw it go over*
>   *all the slobs in Europe were terrified . . .*

The reader has no way of checking Pound's details. It seems
doubtful that the action of the mayor of Wörgl threw all of
European banking into a panic; nor did the ethical fiscal
policies of Athens prevent the ultimate decline of Greek
civilization. Since later in Canto 80 Pound sings a hymn of
hate to celebrate Churchill's electoral defeat, Pound's opinions on Churchill can scarcely be considered the results of
careful examination and impartial historical justice.

Pound's three *exempla* presumably shed intellectual light
on each other. The Greek past says something meaningful to
the twentieth century, makes some ironic comment on present
wickedness. And if some historical lesson can be learned,
something that might move the reader to action, then the
three events must reveal an inner relationship. Does Pound
merely *feel* that the victory at Salamis was the result of moral
banking practices; does Pound *know* that the allied victories
over fascism were engineered by the bankers who were allegedly
"Churchill's backers"? We have, of course, now moved out of
the *Cantos* into actual history and into the problems of
historiography. But Pound keeps nudging the reader out of
his poem and into those areas which asks our questions.

The crucial question is whether the documentary method
is compatible with the ideogrammatic or anachronistic method.
Documents provide the basis for all historiography; they are
the repository of fact and causality, they presumably answer
the pertinent questions of *what, when,* and *how.* But historical
meaning never resides in the documents themselves. As we
work our way through the *Cantos* we learn (as Cassirer points
out) that

>   . . . the facts teach us that history was in reality never
>   anything else but an accumulation of the crimes and
>   misfortunes of the human race. Obviously, the more
>   sharply we scrutinize the parts, the farther we are from a
>   clear comprehension of the whole; on the contrary, it
>   destroys all hope of attaining such understanding.[5]

Cassirer is commenting on Bayle's *Dictionnaire Historique,* a
colossal and fruitless attempt to deduce meaning from a vast

collection of materials. These comments apply to the *Cantos* with uncanny precision. Do not the *Cantos* mean to give us historical understanding based on the hard facts of history itself? Does not Pound offer us, in the original languages and through endless citation, the annals of ancient China, the chronicles of the Borgias and Malatestas, the letters and diaries of the American Founding Fathers, and anecdotes about celebrated literary friends? Pound scrutinizes the parts, believing that history has positive existence in his texts: in his quotations, translations, and in his own uncertain memory.

The meaning of history cannot inhere in unsorted documents and half-remembered gossip. Historical knowledge exists after the application of "some rational discipline or paradigmatic assumption"; the thousands of historical facts (and non-facts) detailed in the *Cantos* form no discernible pattern, no larger structure which becomes epistemologically significant. The method of ideogram and anachronism denies that history requires either verification or chronology; without the possibility of knowing truth from falsehood or what came after when, history is reduced to meaningless recurrence or regressive myth. Ideogram and anachronism deny that history reveals process or that history is available to the understanding. Thus the arrangement (I should say disarrangement) of documentary material in ideograms, in patterns of deliberate chronological disorder, produces nothing we can call historical knowledge.

A controlling power of dialectic and drama might have given Pound's history imaginative shape. The historical content produces no cumulative effect because anachronism sustains the reader in pure present time. History for the *Cantos* never moves either ahead along a line of distinct events or circularly back to some mythic beginning. The ideogrammatic method controverts historical process; the documentary method insists that it is history we are encountering, that this enormous quantity of information and anecdote, of literary paraphrase and current event, must add up to something. If Pound had arranged his material in sharply contrasting thematic groups so that each group had its defined dialectical thrust, then we might experience a sense of process. Or if the

Cantos were vividly dramatic, like the central episodes in *The Waste Land,* we might feel the urgency of Pound's historical pleading. But Pound has neither a sense of dialectic, that ability to handle the philosophical parry and thrust which Eliot displays in *Four Quartets,* nor any sense of the dramatic. There are no memorable *personae* in the *Cantos;* what we remember with unforgettable distinctness is the unending drone of Pound's voice. The lyric voice cannot hold together the thousands of historical moments documented in the poem; it cannot orchestrate the thousands of separate ideograms. Document and ideogram clash but shed no light.

3

Instead of historical process or its analogue, the *Cantos* continually worry (or are worried by) a number of obsessions. An obsession is a trouble in the psyche, an unassuaged and unassuageable mental discomfort. One of Pound's obsessions gropes at the bottom of the ceaselessly flowing stream of human action and comes up with a shining key to The Riddle of History. With this key Pound understands the causes of war and "the most obscure of all the phenomena of history," the downfall of civilizations.[6] Since an obsession is to a viable idea as Sullivan's Lost Chord is to the discoverable clarity of Beethoven's harmonic structure in the Fifth Symphony, we cannot expect Pound to prove his case, that he has indeed discovered the key to History. He merely states it again and again, from the early Cantos to the "Addendum for Canto 100" published in 1968:

> *The Evil is Usury,* neschek
> *the serpent*
> neschek *whose name is known, the defiler,*
> *beyond race and against race*
> *the defiler* . . .

Pound tells us that usury, in its protean manifestations, accounts for men's political crimes as well as for the incompetence and grossness in their works of art. Usury comprehends nearly every variety of human evil. Those who have become unclean through the infection of money are usurers, as are those who prefer making money to making love:

> *And those who had lied for hire;*
> *the perverts, the perverters of language,*
> *the perverts, who have set money-lust*
> *Before the pleasures of the senses . . .*
> *Canto 14*

Usury is the manipulation of money which results in profits for a privileged group at the expense of the community:

> *Belmont representing the Rothschilds*
> *"specie payment's resumption*
> *"enriched a small group of holders."*
> *Canto 40*

Pound frequently touches on traditional Catholic notions of usury. In this passage he invokes natural law in the language of a Church father:

> *Usura slayeth the child in the womb*
> *It stayeth the young man's courting*
> *It hath brought palsey to bed, lyeth*
> *Between the young bride and her bridegroom*
> CONTRA NATURAM
> *Canto 45*

Usury blights love; it marries young girls to rich and impotent old men. Usury, says Aristotle, is the breeding of money with money; and by metaphorical extension, this perverted reproduction affects all natural process. Some of the horror of this practice would be felt by an Elizabethan audience when Antonio and Shylock discuss "usuance":

> ANTONIO: . . . is your gold and silver ewes and rams?
> SHYLOCK: I cannot tell. I make it breed as fast.

This is the medieval concept. Pound pushes it very hard; usury is CONTRA NATURAM because it creates something where nothing existed before:

> *. . . Hath benefit of interest on all*
> *the moneys which it, the bank, creates out of nothing.*
> *Canto 46*

Pound also denounces as usurious the selling of munitions, "superneschek or the international racket." Pound holds to the popular notion of the twenties and thirties that wars are deliberately arranged and staged by international bankers and the sellers of munitions. We can follow through the *Cantos* the adventures of those who start wars for profit; they are the "real" forces in history:

> *War, one war after another,*
> *Men start 'em who couldn't put up a good hen-roost.*
> > Canto 18

> > "Will there be war? "No, Miss Wi'let,
> > "On account of bizschniz relations."
> > > Canto 38

> *Said Herr Krupp (1842): guns are a merchandise*
> *I approach them from the industrial end,*
> *I approach them from the technical side.*
> > Canto 38

> *Pus was in Spain, Wellington was a jew's pimp*
> *and lacked mind to know what he effected.*
> *"Leave the Duke, Go for gold!"*
> *In their souls was usura and in their hearts*
> *cowardice . . .*
> > Canto 50

Early in the *Cantos* we encounter Zennos Metevsky, who is a thinly disguised Basil Zaharoff. The name of Zaharoff itself occurs later in Canto 93:

> *Taffy went putty-colour when I mentioned Zaharoff (1914)*
> *And general Whoosis, when he read the name,*
> > *Aquarone,*
> > > *30 years later*
> *or as Ub said: "ten to charge a nest of machine guns*
> *for one who will put his name on a chit."*
> > Canto 93

Metevsky-Zaharoff moves from one country to another, exerting his malevolent influence. He, too, is a usurer because he trades money for human life.

Pound's idea of usury is broad and inclusive. It is also highly idiosyncratic, bearing little resemblance to what historians and theoreticians have said about the development of modern banking and commercial enterprise. *Usury* is a dirty word with which Pound indicts munitions-selling, fiscal systems, and the complex politics of modern Europe. Pound's "study" of economics supposedly traces the deterioration of culture brought about by the abrogation of the traditional theological strictures against usury; it also traces the ways in which the corruption spread from social practice to the forms of art. However, Pound demonstrates no relationships between art and economics or between economics and politics. We must accept Pound's word that whatever is evil in the modern world is the result of usurious practices. Pound's theory is single, simple, and unequivocal; the history of western Europe and America, in all its variousness and complexity, can be understood if we recognize usury as the motivation behind human action.

Even if we find some truth in Pound's *ad hoc* definition of usury (munitions-selling *is* a despicable racket), its application is irresponsible and dangerous. Doctrines of historical decay, as we noted earlier, link themselves with racial thinking; Pound cannot resist the temptation to pin the decline of the west on the Jews. He tries to make a qualifying distinction between "good" and "bad" Jews:

> . . . *sin drawing vengeance, poor yitts paying for*
> *paying for a few big jews' vendetta on goyim* . . .

but such a distinction, couched in such offensive language, hardly mitigates the obscenity of the attitude. During the unfortunate Bollingen Award controversy, much was made of Pound's anti-Semitism. Anti-Semitism was named "a governing myth of the *Cantos*." But anti-Semitism cannot be a governing myth in a poem without governing myths at all. Rather, Pound's allegations about Jews appear as dirty asides, whispers into the reader's ear reporting the inside dope about History.

Pound's application of "economics" to provide the key to History carries with it the heavy flavor of the nineteenth century. Doctrines of historical decline and decay were popularized in the writings of Gobineau and in the political scribblings of Richard Wagner. Marx also provided the fullest, and philosophically the most respectable, economic interpretation of history. But Pound's understanding of usury never reaches factual precision or philosophical refinement; it is an overwhelming sentiment rather than a critical passion. To believe in a "key to History," to believe that a single historical phenomenon explains historical process means holding one of the many varieties of conspiratorial theories of history. And a conspiratorial theory of history can hardly "affirm the gold thread in the pattern. . . ."

4

Programmatic anachronism destroys the form of historical process; the obsession with usury gives it only the most spurious content. Certainly "a poem containing history" must have its possible container, an intellectual system (which is also a metaphorical system) which encloses it. We have described time as the container for the thing contained and the thing contained as history. Anachronism of course denies the validity of the container; Pound discovers early in the *Cantos* that "Time is the evil." The enemy is not usury, corrupt politics, or fiscal incompetence; the enemy is time. Pound's loveliest episodes exploit the pathos of mutability and rage against time's depredations:

> *We also made ghostly visits, and the stair*
> *That knew us, found us again on the turn of it,*
> *Knocking at empty rooms, seeking for buried beauty;*
> *But the sun-tanned, gracious and well-formed fingers*
> *Lift no latch of bent bronze, no Empire handle*
> *Twists for the knocker's fall; no voice to answer.*
> *A strange concierge, in place of the gouty-footed.*
> *Sceptic against all this one seeks the living,*
> *Stubborn against the fact. The wilted flowers*
> *Brushed out a seven year since, of no effect.*
> *Damn the partition! Paper, dark brown and stretched,*
> *Flimsy and damned partition.*
>   *Ione, dead the long year*
> *My lintel, and Liu Ch'e's lintel.*
> *Time blacked out with the rubber.*
>
>   *Canto 7*

This passage handles, in an exquisite shift of rhythms, the conventional theme of *ubi sunt*. The feeling is never deep but (as Austin Warren says of Hopkins) "hovers closely over the text, the linguistic surface."

The lyric evocation of time's ravages is a persistent and traceable musical fragment in the *Cantos*. If the poem is about anything at all, it is about how time kills beauty, how

> *Les moeurs passent et la douleur reste . . .*

Pound's feelings about time and mutability never rise to any height of metahistorical grandeur; his feelings are personal, never directed toward apocalypse or toward eternity, a world without time. He sadly admits his inability to comprehend eschatological hopes:

> *I don't know how humanity stands it*
> *With a painted paradise at the end of it*
> *without a painted paradise at the end of it*
> *Canto 74*

Without either a religious or secular eschatology, we have nothing the mind can understand as historical process. But change is always apparent, always inevitable, always terrifying. Pound reiterates throughout the *Cantos* Heraclitus's mysterious fragment πάντα ῥεῖ "Everything flows":

> *Uncle George stood like a statesman* 'PEI ΠΑΝΤΑ
> *fills up every hollow*
> *the cake shops in the Nevsky, and Schöners*
> *not to mention der Greif at Bolsano . . .*
> *Canto 74*

> *for those trees are Elysium*
> *for serenity*
> *under Abelard's bridges* πάντα ῥεῖ
> *for those trees are serenity . . .*
> *Canto 80*

> *PANTA 'REI, said DuBellay translating*
> *the base shall we say, and the slide of Byzantium,*
> *bags, baskets full of, presumably, coinage,*
> *and lured twenty thousand sclavons.*
> *Canto 96*

The long flank, the firm breast
and to know beauty and death and despair
and to think that what has been shall be,
flowing, ever unstill.

Canto 113

It would be quite impossible to cite all the passages which express Pound's elegiac recollections, fear of the temporal process, or bafflement with the cruel fact that things and people change and that the present so quickly dissolves into the past. Art can comfort, can erect a veil between ceaseless change and the poet's sensibility; brilliant and beautiful images flash through the darkness of the overwhelming night of time:

These concepts the human mind has attained.
To make Cosmos—
Muss., wrecked for an error,
But the record
      the palimpsest—
a little light
      in great darkness—

Canto 116

The light has its power of occasional illumination. It shows Pound puzzling over his own past actions, wondering about his poem, and hoping something can be saved from the ruins of time.

Despite Pound's awareness of time passing, he reveals nothing in the *Cantos* we might call temporal process. Some critics have discovered in the *Cantos* evidence that Pound holds a cyclical concept of time or that Pound progresses *through* time: from the writhing disorder and hate of an *Inferno* to the blessed order and love of a *Paradiso*. But these integrative critics write in their criticism the poem Pound might have written but could not. If the *Cantos* demonstrate the circularity of time and history, we should be be able to discern some leading myth of recurrence; the events in the poem should be points along the circumference of a clearly drawn circle. The beginning and end would meet like the serpent devouring his tail. As the poem now stands, Canto I begins with Pound's englishing of Andreas Divus' Homer, Odysseus' descent into Hell; Canto 117, a fragment, tells of shattered dreams and quixotic struggle against evil:

> M'amour, m'amour
> > what do I love and
> > where are you?
> That I lost my center
> > fighting the world.
> The dreams clash
> > and are shattered—
> and that I tried to make a paradiso
> > terrestre.

Canto 117 shows neither a return to beginnings nor a resolution in time or out of it.

The *Cantos* is not a poem sustained by circular or organic time: by myths of death and resurrection or by the return of the seasons. Quite deliberately the *Cantos* is a poem without time or sequence; it would make no difference if we started with Canto 50 and read backwards to Canto 1; or if we read only the even or odd Cantos. If the poem were sustained by an integrating myth, there would be a discoverable movement—from birth to death and resurrection; or from winter to spring. What sustains the Cantos, in those places where we can follow Pound's meanings and respond to his feelings, is tone and mood; the binding material is the pervading emotions of regret and despair. Pound's understanding of time and history is limited to his own feelings. He knows that events took place, that men and women suffered, that it all seems a terrifying waste. Time and history are thus reduced to a spectacle of undifferentiated change—a spectacle where all event is inexplicable occurrence:

> Ignez da Castro murdered, and a wall
> Here stripped, here made to stand.
> Drear waste, the pigment flakes from the stone,
> Or plaster flakes, Mantegna painted the wall.
> Silk tatters, "Nec Spe Nec Metu."
> > > > Canto 3

5

Perhaps the *Cantos* do not belong in this study. The poem is incomplete and Pound is not likely to revise or complete it.

Since the poem denies the existence of historical process and
makes deliberate disorder of historical knowledge, what can
my particular critical perspective show? Only negative findings,
I fear. The poem in the context of this study is an example
of what happens when an artist neither discovers nor controls
his subject. We know Pound's intentions: that history, in all its
immense variety, could provide the *Cantos* with both structure
and meaning; that the finished poem could provide a solution
to the problems of a decayed civilization and a corrupt social
order. We cannot deny the importance of Pound's theme to
our century. Milton's theodicy and Dante's journey from
damnation to salvation were of similar importance to their
centuries. *Paradise Lost* and *The Divine Comedy* saw the
problems of human existence transcended in the light of religious revelation. Pound reasoned as a good historicist: we
no longer have religion but we have History. History can save
us; this is the rationale underlying Pound's concern.

History cannot save us, however, unless we know what it is
and how we can use it. History without chronology, without
an understanding of cause and effect, is not an intellectual
form. An obsession, Pound's alleged conspiracy of usurers
mocks responsible historiography. The assumption that all
history is contemporaneous allows Pound to think about usury
in any way he wishes. If we discard chronology and causation,
any idea (and usury is an idea) can be juggled and applied to
the most unrelated circumstance. Nor can we dismiss or ignore
Pound's ideas as harmless literary fictions. The *Cantos* insist
that our world has been made rotten with usury; the poem
means to educate the reader in right thinking and ultimately
in right action. Perhaps no poet since Shelley has had such
a sanguine view of the moral effects of poetry. That Pound's
purpose is nearly obscured in his ruined depository of documents is doubtless a blessing.

An ideogrammatic and anachronistic historiography is not
history but a technique for confusion. Ideogram ostensibly releases poetry from the shackles of rational syntax; anachronism
releases the event from the pattern and teleology of historical
process. Actually, in proposing the literal simultaneity of all
events, ideogram and anachronism sever human connections
with the past and negate the idea of a future. In their

timeless, a-syntactical present, the *Cantos* despair of history; history is somehow *there* in the creating mind of the poet; but devoid of relationship and purpose, we cannot know it, understand it, or make judgments about it. And Pound's discovery of "the real basis" of history, economics, is hardly original. Marx and his followers long ago gave coherent intellectual expression to the doctrine that political economy was the infrastructure upon which all cultural superstructures were erected. Pound's obsession with usury reduces to a vulgar absurdity Marx's analysis of capitalism; ironically Pound acknowledges Marx in a condescending sneer:

> . . . *Mr Marx, Karl, did not*
> *foresee this conclusion, you have seen a good deal of*
> *the evidence, not knowing it evidence* . . .
>
> *Canto 46*

When we consider Pound's contempt for systematic historiography and his willingness to admit into the *Cantos* forgery and vulgar prejudice as "evidence"—we understand that Pound holds an anti-intellectual view of history. Such "history" is immensely popular, and Pound's acceptance of it can be explained by his desire to shock respectability, to thumb his nose at conventional attitudes and orthodox opinion. He always felt that his country and his age rejected him and that he was not sufficiently acknowledged as an artist and social thinker. By offering his own idiosyncratic History as the lowdown about men and their affairs, he affirmed his own position as moralist and thinker. If the Establishment refused his politics and poetry, he then wrote a History which overturns conventional notions of chronology, motivation, and cause.

Important political implications emerge from a view of history which is willing to see historical order destroyed, which accepts forgery and crackpot notion, and which rewrites the past. Totalitarian propaganda also undertook the radical revision of history in accordance with totalitarian political needs. Such "history" disowned the truth, substituted demonology for analysis and judgment, and utterly simplified historical cause. Such "history" appeared plausible and attractive to an intellectual elite who were disgusted with academicism and bourgeois hypocrisy. Members of this elite could "get back at the Establishment" by discrediting conventional judgments and the scholars' estimation of history. Hannah Arendt remarks:

> The members of the elite did not object at all to paying a price, the destruction of civilization, for the fun of seeing how those who had been excluded unjustly in the past forced their way into it. They were not particularly outraged at the monstrous forgeries in historiography of which all totalitarian regimes are guilty and which announce themselves clearly enough in totalitarian propaganda. They had convinced themselves that traditional historiography was a forgery in any case, since it excluded the underprivileged and oppressed from the memory of mankind.[7]

Pound's career exhibits what Miss Arendt calls "the temporary alliance between the mob and the elite." It also exhibits that alliance between aestheticism and barbarism which Mann castigates in *Doctor Faustus*. Like Daniel zur Höhe—Mann's portrait of Ludwig Derleth, a ferocious disciple of Stefan George—Pound set himself up as a warrior of art, issuing manifestoes and orders of the day. After his early flirtation with *fin-de-siècle* decadence, he moved into politics where he wore the masks of primitive and revolutionary. He entered what Mann called "the old-new world of revolutionary reaction": the world of right-wing political extremism. Fascism satisfied Pound's taste for violence and uninhibited rhetoric. Mussolini plays a heroic role in Pound's History, ranking with Confucius in wisdom and with Thomas Jefferson in political skill.

At this late date it may seem a matter of pumping bullets into a dead lion to speak of Pound's fascism. Indeed, tasteful critics now hardly mention it; Daniel D. Pearlman's book-length study of the *Cantos, The Barb of Time,* blithely accepts without critical demurrer Pound's equation of Mussolini and Jefferson. Mr. Pearlman also wonders why Pound shows such hostility to Einstein, remarking "Of course there is no direct relationship intended between usury and Einstein, but Einstein does nevertheless become a convenient 'symbol' for all that is wrong in the West."[8] Perhaps Mr. Pearlman does not know that Einstein was a Jew; for Pound this would connect him with usury and the downfall of the West.

I am indiscreet enough to mention Pound's political attitudes because they bear directly on Pound's History and his idea of culture. For Pound's History junks the past as the totalitarian rewriting of conventional history does; the ideo-grammatic method quite effectively renders history unintelligible. Pound's idea of culture looks toward a primitive Eden, toward an essentially *uncivilized* world:

> *Sun up; work*
> *sundown; to rest*
> *dig well and drink of the water*
> *dig field; eat of the grain*
> *Imperial power is? and to us what is it?*
> *Canto 49*

The *persona* here (an Eskimo?) speaks nonsyntactical or pidgin English. He lives *das simpel Leben* in accordance with nature and organic time. Despite Pound's avowals that the *Cantos* were written to reaffirm Western culture, his social primitivism suggests that hostility to culture which Freud remarked as a besetting danger to the modern world.

I am not using the word culture in its arts-and-humanities sense. Pound is a learned and cultivated connoisseur of all the arts. But in both his political attachments and in the *Cantos* Pound waged a furious campaign against the bourgeois tradition, rational historiography, and anything that might be considered conventional or not sufficiently revolutionary. Always in the avant-garde, he proclaimed as his motto "Make it new!" Always the enthusiast for the latest movement, he urged the demolition of the nineteenth century—that good gray century of middle-class values. A scholar and intellectual himself, he sneered at scholars and intellectuals; in his own frivolous way, he reached for a revolver when he heard the word culture: he spelled it Kulchur. Pound was not alone in thinking that it might be fun to blow up the European cultural heritage; the Futurists and Dadaists showed a similar taste for what they felt was "creative" violence.

In all his activities Pound was neither consistent nor aware that at one and the same time he was urging the destruction of culture and thinking himself the last defender of Europe and the West. Nor was he aware that in pushing his campaign against history (for that is what the *Cantos* do), he became an enemy of the Europe he believed he was defending. At this point I am tempted to say that Pound's History, with its thousands of documents, letters, and economics of social credit; with its Greek, Latin, and Chinese words of wisdom; is, in the words of another American primitive, The Bunk. Perhaps Pound cannot be dismissed so glibly. It took tremendous effort and the work of more than fifty years to write the one hundred and seventeen Cantos; it has taken the work of a dozen critics to discover their form and unravel their obscurities. The *Cantos* is the longest modern poem in English; it offered itself as a solution to the problems of its age. Yet the *Cantos* remains an unsuccessful epic of human culture (more exactly, an epic against culture) because it is based on an idea of history and a historiographical method to which the mind, unless it abrogates its responsibility, cannot give assent.

VI

André Malraux

"But when the soul fades, what appears in its place: action, or the calling in question of life by death?"
—André Malraux, *Anti-Memoirs*

I

Gerontion dreams on History, remaining powerless to change what he fears and abhors. He is a witness who interprets the world but cannot transform it: a prophet who speculates on "the end of the event" but does not participate in action. Malraux's protagonists seize History by the throat and engage the world in deadly encounter. For them History is embodied in war and revolution; their dream does not focus on the fragmented past but on the *hic et nunc* of present realities and a future which promises a society released from the humiliations of poverty and subjugation. It would be feeble to say Malraux treats "the problem of history." His novels assert that History is human destiny; that revolution is the authentic and "real" form of the historical process; that the individual will must come to terms with the fatalism of History. Thus we discover in Malraux not only the questions we have so far considered— the value of historical knowledge and the nature of historical process—but a shifting complex of ideological positions which sometimes emerge as political doctrine, at other times as the severest questioning of political doctrine.

The ideological positions dramatized in the novels bear a close relationship to Malraux's personal commitments during his novel-writing years. He was a man of the Left (but not a Communist party-member)[1] until the beginning of the Second World War. As a young man he joined the Communist-led Jeune-Annam movement and helped to edit its Saigon newspaper, *L'Indochine*. In the mid-twenties he journeyed to China and played a mysterious role in the left wing of the Kuomintang. Whether he was an agent of the Kuomintang or worked in their propaganda bureau or whether he participated, in even a minor way, in the revolutionary actions described in *The Conquerors* and *Man's Fate,* is highly doubtful; his recently published *Anti-Memoirs* (1967–68) is brilliantly evasive and does little to clarify and much to enlarge the mythical dimensions of Malraux's early life. (The *Anti-Memoirs* indicate that Malraux has either forgotten how or never learned to speak Chinese; in a recent official visit to China, he communicates with Chou En-lai and Mao through an interpreter.) During the thirties Malraux was a dedicated anti-Fascist. He wrote polemics against Mussolini and Hitler, agitated against Nazi atrocities, and raised money for Popular Front causes. He served in Spain and organized the International Air Squadron. When the Second World War broke out, he enlisted in an armored unit, was captured by the Germans, escaped, and during 1941–45 fought in the Resistance. He came out of the war an admirer and supporter of de Gaulle; since 1948 he has pursued a vigorous anti-Communist political line.

Malraux's very public and well-publicized political life has misled some of his readers into understandable errors about the ideological content of his novels. Trotsky admired what he felt were the purely literary virtues of Malraux's first novel, *The Conquerors,* but faulted Malraux and his hero Garine for not understanding the true nature of revolution:

> A solid inoculation of Marxism might have protected the author from fatal mistakes. . . . But Garine, on the whole, considers revolutionary doctrine to be "doctrinal rubbish." He is, as we see, one of those for whom the Revolution is only an "established state of affairs." Is this not remarkable? It is precisely because the Revolution is a "state of affairs"—that is, a stage in the develop-

ment of a society conditioned by objective causes and subject to established laws—that a scientific mind can foresee
the general direction of the process. Only through the
study of the anatomy and physiology of society can one
act on the current of events, basing oneself on scientific
forecasts, not on dilettantist conjectures.[2]

Garine, Trotsky complains, is a bad revolutionary because
he does not possess "a scientific mind [that can] foresee the
general direction of the process." Because Garine refuses to
subject himself to correct ideological discipline, Garine cannot truly personify the Marxist faith that History moves in-
exorably toward its triumphant conclusion in a communist
society. In his reply to Trotsky, Malraux is too polite to point
out that Trotsky's unflinching doctrinal orthodoxy did not
prevent him from making "fatal mistakes"; although Malraux
cannot resist mentioning "[Trotsky] thinks that Garine is
wrong; but Stalin thinks that he, Trotsky, is wrong."

Neither Garine nor his creator believe that History
marches in the ranks of true Marxist believers; no "proper"
political attitude can guarantee the successful outcome of
events. Malraux's characters engage History not as mechanical
agents in a prepared scenario but as fallible beings caught up
in tragic action. Those who take part in the historical drama,
who commit themselves (in Malraux's celebrated phrase)
"to the test of action," discover no infallible method which
saves them from the unprecedented exigencies of historical
reality. The Cunning of Reason defeats, deflects, or betrays
those who think they know "the general direction of the
process"; those who act in blissful ignorance; and those who
make revolution for the hell of it.

If Malraux espouses no orthodox program of revolutionary
behavior, his characters do act within a context of shifting
and provisional attitudes toward the historical process—the
great sweep of events and the power which seems to impel
them. Garine, although obsessed with the idea of revolution,
is no *apparatnik*. What drives him to action on behalf of the
revolutionary movement is richly contradictory, that is, funda-
mentally confused and *human*. At times he talks the rhetoric
of heroic disinterestedness: "My strength comes from my being

absolutely unscrupulous in the service of something other than my own immediate interest." Earlier Malraux characterizes Garine as an embodiment of a Nietzschean will-to-power:

> . . . like a disease, persistent, tenacious, he felt within him a craving for power . . . for its own sake, not for the wealth, notoriety or respect it might bring. If, in some moment of childish fancying, he ever dreamed of power, it was in a manner almost physical—not in the least romantic, but with a tension of his whole being, like that of a beast preparing to pounce on his prey; and this led him to regard the actual exercise of power as a kind of relief, a deliverance.

Nietzsche more than Marx establishes the ideological basis of *The Conquerors*. Garine's revolutionary dedication takes the form of a *willed* encounter with History; it is struggle which interests him and History provides a destiny to which he can submit himself. He neither loves mankind nor believes in the moral superiority of the downtrodden. When the revolution triumphs and the masses assume power, "they will become contemptible. . . . All we have in common is our struggle, that is the one thing which is clear." *Amor fati* is also Garine's motto; ill with fever, he murmurs: "Ah! that intangible something which makes a man feel that his life is dominated by some force. . . ." History and its violence provide that intangible something, that dynamic fatalism which gives living its urgency and excitement. Garine wishes to embrace History, to move when it moves, and if he is destroyed in "the test of action," all well and good; he will have fulfilled not only his own destiny but, linking himself with the revolutionary movement of the masses, he will have shared a common fate.

Garine's *amor fati* reaches metaphysical levels. Violent deeds, the excitements of combat and command, the developing hysteria of a city under the stress of events it slowly comes to grasp: these impinge on Garine's consciousness with the force of a religious revelation. What men once sought in religious belief—a moral order, a way to bring the chaos of life under some control, a plan for future salvation—Garine seeks in the labyrinths of History. As a young man he has suffered humiliation through unjust imprisonment; he has been deeply injured and suffers the sting of *ressentiment*. Alvear, the skeptical intellectual of Malraux's later novel *Man's Hope,* offers a character analysis of the Garine type of revolutionary:

> Hope "springs eternal" as they say, and it's a terrifying thing! A man who has been unjustly sentenced, or has run up against more than his share of ingratitude or baseness or stupidity—well, he's bound to stake his hope on some new order. Among other functions, the revolution plays a part that an "eternal life" used formerly to play; that explains many of its characteristics.

Garine knows, of course, that there is no salvation in events themselves; he also knows the end of the action always remains in doubt. Futility and uncertainty screw up the tension; his interest is something of a gambler's interest: "If I readily threw in my lot with the Revolution it was because its results are remote and uncertain. At bottom, I am a gambler. . . ." His intellect tells him he will probably lose the game against History; the cards are stacked and the play is wild. But as a Nietzschean, he believes intellect must retreat before life and life can be felt only in frenzied activity.

Garine's attachment to the life of action is undercut by a pervading inner anguish. Knowledge may be evaded in deeds; the symptoms of a diseased subjectivity ignored or suppressed in the heat of battle. But Garine's individuality, which he offers to the objective force of History, paradoxically enlarges and mounts as he seemingly succeeds in bending events to his will. Through sudden executions of brutal policy, acts of instant justice, and brilliantly intuitive strategy, Garine actually brings the revolutionary action to the point of success. As he succeeds, his inner doubt and confusion mount; he is ill with fever and will eventually die of it. His illness is a given of the novel but Malraux heavily suggests that it issues from an existential despair. Toward the end of the book, Garine announces, "There can be no strength, there cannot be any *real life* without the conviction, without the obsession of the futility of everything." His disgust increases as he becomes an Unhappy Consciousness, estranged from the "insufferable Bolshevik mentality, this stupid glorification of discipline . . . ," from the idea of Revolution, from the horror and violence inevitably occasioned by historical eruptions. In one of his final outbursts, he announces the desire to go to England, "To England. Now that I know what Empire is—one tenacious, constant act of violence. To direct, to determine, to constrain. That is life."

While the will-to-power motivates Garine, power itself ultimately breeds within him a sense of loathing, that familiar nausea which afflicts the spiritually bankrupt heroes of Sartre and Camus. Garine is horrified at the methods both the enemy and he himself employ: the use of torture, mutilation, and the deliberate degrading of human beings. He quarrels with Borodin, the Soviet organizer and representative of the International. His resistance to Communist ideology and his knowledge that the revolution will be betrayed both by wicked men and the irreconcilable differences within the Communist-Kuomintang coalition contribute to his profound belief in the "futility of everything." But metaphysical discontent unnerves him as much as political disputes. At the source of his despair works the virus of daydreaming which earlier had provoked him to a life of action; it also infects him with a sense of isolation from those events which ostensibly justify his humanity but more nearly consume it.

2

Man's Fate enlarges and deepens the thematic concerns of *The Conquerors.* What in the earlier work is confused or aborted ("the work of an adolescent," Malraux himself judged in 1948)[3] now emerges with startling lucidity. From the perspective of this study, the theme of *Man's Fate* is the tragic discrepancy between human intention and historical outcome; between what man's will attempts with all the passion of intellect, feeling, and desire and what emerges in "the desolation of reality." Kyo, who is not so much spokesman for Malraux's position in *Man's Fate* as his mediator among a number of positions, opts for will, albeit with a certain amount of caution: "But in Marxism there is the sense of fatality, and also the exaltation of a will. Every time fatality comes before will I'm suspicious." Here Kyo is arguing with the Soviet functionary Vologin who urges that the Shanghai revolutionaries surrender their arms, cooperate with Chiang Kai-shek, and submit to party discipline in all matters of political policy. Vologin formulates his position within an orthodox Marxist context; the Revolution *is* fatality and cannot help being born into historical reality. He theorizes, "By its very nature [the Revolution] must become socialist. We must let it find its own way. Our job is to safeguard its birth. And not to abort it."

Vologin is not an evil man; his misinterpretation of the military and political situation is based on poor information and a Westerner's inability to understand China. Kyo has better information, knows the importance of the Chinese peasantry, understands what motivates both worker and peasant in an undeveloped country; and events prove Kyo correct. But the conflict between Kyo and Vologin poses more than a question of tactics; it reaches deep into one of those unsolved and insoluble contradictions which animates Marx's theory of history. On the one hand Marx accepted Hegel's eschatological vision of world-history moving toward higher and higher states of realized existence. The power to transform world-history would be supplied by the overthrow of the existing social order, by the communist revolution. Revolution was inevitable, a fatality; and for orthodox Marxists the Revolution is still an article of Messianic faith which no events in actual history can shatter. On the other hand, only men can make a revolution: "History is nothing but the activity of men in pursuit of their own ends." Men create themselves through their own labor, "*History* does nothing. . . ."[4]

The tension between the fatalism of history and "the activity of men in pursuit of their own ends" sustains both ideology and structure in *Man's Fate*. Ferral, the capitalist and erotomaniac, and Vologin, the Comintern bureaucrat, make their particular appeals to history and the life of action. Vologin holds faith with the party-line interpretation of history and helps betray the Shanghai uprising to Chiang Kai-shek. Ferral makes the most impassioned plea that "A man is the sum of his actions, of what he has *done,* of what he can do. Nothing else." Vologin, like many of his comrades, is tricked by The Cunning of Reason—that higher purpose of the

Dialectic which always remains concealed to human vision. Ferral thinks that he is the sum of his actions, that he creates himself in the pursuit of his own capitalist ends. But his will-to-power is not generated by conscious volition alone; he is created as much by his uncontrollable obsessions—emblematized by his need to humiliate women—as he is by his financial enterprises.

Man's Fate is a richer, denser book than *The Conquerors*. Malraux abandons the panoramic, newsreel method of depicting immediate history (he returns to it in *Man's Hope*) and preserves an almost classical unity of time and place. There is no privileged narrator; Malraux tells his story from the "omniscient author point of view": from inside the varied experiences of a carefully selected cast of characters. This dividing of consciousness allows a "truer" depiction of the complexities of a historical event as it is being formed. Just as Pierre Bezukhov cannot grasp what is happening at the battle of Borodino, so neither Kyo nor Ch'en, neither the buffoon Clappique nor the manic Ferral, ever grasp the total meaning of the revolution which both controls and is controlled by their actions. Each character affects some part of the outcome but the outcome contradicts expectation. Each character pursues his private interests: his political idealism, his obsessions with women or opium, his distractions or his whimsies. Hate, fear, the need for revenge are all part of the process. But the process is also shaped and moved by that metaphysical agent History, the principle of fate or destiny—essentially unknown and unknowable.

At the level of theory, the problems of historical causation remain insoluble. Malraux wisely refrains from imposing authorial interpretations on events; he allows his characters to theorize but they do so largely *in character*. Vologin enunciates the party-line which History then proceeds to discredit; Katov tries out various ideological positions largely for Kyo's benefit—to cheer him up, as it were. Vologin is a humorless functionary from whom we would expect elaborate theoretical rationalization. Katov is not an intellectual and his discomfort with ideology is almost comic. Malraux's concerns emerge from entire passages, from the clash of opposing characters, from the conflicting claims of friendship and tactical necessity, and from the symbolic resonances of language and scene.

The following passage occurs toward the end of Part Two. An officer from the Kuomintang has informed Kyo, Katov, and Ch'en that the workers' militia must surrender their arms to Chiang Kai-shek. Kyo telephones Comintern headquarters at Hankow. The international urges Kyo to cooperate with Chiang. The officer leaves.

"Are you willing that we should give up the arms?" Kyo asked Katov.

"I'm trying to understand. Before anything else, we must go to Hankow, you see. What does the Int'rnational want? First of all, use the army of the Kuomintang to unify China. After that d'velop the Rev'lution by prop'-ganda and the rest. It must change of its own accord from a dem'cratic Rev'lution into a socialist Rev'lution."

"Chiang Kai-shek must be killed," said Ch'en.

"Chiang Kai-shek will no longer allow us to go as far as that," answered Kyo, ignoring Ch'en's remark. "He cannot. He can maintain himself here only by drawing on the customs and the contributions of the bourgeoisie, and the bourgeoisie won't pay for nothing: he will have to pay them back with the corpses of Communists."

"All that," said Ch'en, "means nothing."

"Leave us alone," said Katov. "You don't think you're going to try to kill Chiang Kai-shek without the consent of the Central Committee, or at least the delegate of the Int'rnational?"

A distant rumble gradually filled the silence.

"You're going to Hankow?" Ch'en asked Kyo.

"Naturally."

Ch'en was pacing back and forth in the room, beneath all the pendulums and balance-wheels of the various time-pieces which went on ticking their measure.

"What I have said is very simple," he said at last. "The essential. The only thing to do. Let them know."

"Will you wait?"

Kyo knew that if Ch'en hesitated instead of answering, it was not because Katov had convinced him. It was be-cause none of the present orders of the International satisfied the profound passion which had made him a revolutionary; if he accepted them, through discipline, he would no longer be able to act. Kyo watched that hostile figure beneath the clocks: he had made the sacrifice of himself and of others to the Revolution, and now the Revolution would perhaps throw him back into his solitude with his memories of assassinations. At once with him and against him, Kyo could no longer either join him nor break with him.

Katov, who is "trying to understand," has been through the Russian Revolution and appeals to certain historical precedents. History has behaved in such a way during the events of 1917; present political reality must be tested against the revolutionary experience of the past. He wishes to collaborate with History but he is not an opportunist like Vologin and the Moscow bureaucrats. He seeks nothing for himself and does not put ideology before humanity. His revolutionary concern shows the disinterestedness of the professional; he takes a primary interest in tactics and organization. His are, in effect, military virtues; he wants to defeat the enemies of the Revolution not on ideological but real battlefields. After he is captured, he maintains a high level of *esprit de corps;* his jaunty mode of expression and his cheerfulness would be almost offensive—if they were not redeemed by his final, overwhelming act of self-sacrifice.

In the passage above, Katov also plays tunes on the party-line. He is trying to convince himself as well as Kyo that History might be on the side of the Moscow tacticians. Kyo has the political sophistication that Katov and Ch'en lack; he also speaks with the wisdom of Malraux's hindsight. (*Man's Fate* appeared in 1933, some six years after the Shanghai uprising.) While Katov fumbles toward understanding, Kyo penetrates to the heart of the matter. Chiang Kai-shek will collaborate with the moneyed powers: he must pay his soldiers and buy arms. After he secures Shanghai with the help of the Communist militia, he will turn on the Communists. Kyo has privileged knowledge; he sees with clarity the end of the event. Unable to convince the Moscow authorities, Kyo nevertheless pushes on to that disastrous end and to his own death.

In the colloquy with Katov and Ch'en, Kyo finds himself between the level-headed professionalism of Katov and the disturbing insistencies of Ch'en. Ch'en, in many ways the most intriguing character in *Man's Fate,* is a soul sickened by his inner despair and what he must do to overcome it. He serves the Revolution not out of political interest but out of the need to overcome his estrangement. Katov and Kyo can endure the violence they both sustain and commit because the goal of the Revolution transcends all injury to themselves and others. The idea of Revolution brings men into a present community of shared interest; men who already possess a sense of vocation band together to overturn an unjust social order. The utopian ideal of a renovated society sustains those who create themselves through what they do with their hands or think with their minds. Although Ch'en makes revolution in behalf of the workers, he cannot identify with their present activity or share in their hope for their future:

> A man pulled a bicycle from inside the truck, and left. Ch'en recognized him as he was getting on: Ma, one of the principal agitators. . . . A typographer, who had devoted his whole life, since the age of twelve to creating Unions of printshop workers everywhere, with the hope of organizing all Chinese typographers; tried, condemned to death, a fugitive, still organizing. Shouts of joy: the men had recognized him at the same moment as Ch'en, and were acclaiming him. He looked at them. The world they were preparing condemned him—Ch'en—as much as did that of their enemies. What would he do in the factory of the future that lay hidden behind their blue blouses?

Ma is bound to the world as a worker and organizer; Ch'en, without vocation, seeks to overcome his estrangement through killing. And he terrifies himself with the realization that in a perverse and horrible way assassination is becoming his *métier, his* vocation: not a means for creating but for destroying himself.

We see Ch'en at the very opening of *Man's Fate* preparing to kill a sleeping man. In the breathless, otherworldly atmosphere of this scene, every detail of objective reality and of Malraux's close analysis of Ch'en's mounting anguish contribute to the illusion that time has ceased and the ordinary world, governed by clocks and calendars, no longer exists. And in Ch'en's last appearance, as he puts a revolver into his mouth and drifts off in a haze of pain and death, the illusion of his temporal transcendence is complete. He expires in what can only be described as an ecstasy of pain: "Everything was turning, slowly and inevitably, along a great circle—and yet nothing existed but pain." At these stunning moments Ch'en is redeemed from the world of disorderly process and unprecedented event.

Nietzsche again comes to mind. Ch'en is condemned to repeat his acts; as he deliberately wounds himself for the second time by driving a fragment of glass into his thigh, he thinks, "One always does the same thing . . ." His actions move outward from his compulsions—along Zarathustra's "long shuddering street" of the Eternal Recurrence—and return him where he started. We see him first in the act of killing a man; we see him for the last time killing himself. Malraux invests each scene of killing with the high excitement of a religious rite; Ch'en calls to mind a neophyte priest presiding at some Dionysian ceremony of ordained violence. Ch'en's actions and obsessions indeed issue from injured religious sensibility; he is a lapsed Christian and his encounter with the preacher Smithson, on the afternoon before his self-immolation, underlines both his apostasy and his residue of baffled religious feeling.

Another martyr driven by an injured religious sensibility seems to have served Malraux as a model for Ch'en. Kirilov, Peter Verkhovensky's fall guy in *The Possessed,* also wishes to live in an eternal present. This passage, in which Stavrogin is catechizing Kirilov, bears heavily on Malraux's conception; Stavrogin speaks first and Kirilov responds:[5]

> "Have you come to believe in a future, eternal life then?"
>
> "No, not in a future, eternal life, but in this present, eternal life. There are moments—you can reach moments—when time suddenly stops and becomes eternal."
>
> "And you hope to reach such a moment?"
>
> "I do."
>
> "It's hardly likely in our time," Stavrogin said slowly and thoughtfully, also without irony. "In the Apocalypse, the angel promises that there'll be no more time."

"I know. There's a lot of truth in it; it's clear and precise. When man attains happiness, there will be no more time because there will be no need for it. It's a very true thought."

"Where will they hide time?"

"Nowhere. Time is not a thing, it's an idea. It will vanish from the mind."

Ch'en, like Kirilov, yearns for apocalypse, *that there be no more time*. He seeks happiness, a release from his absolute alienation, in performing the most extreme of acts—in committing murder. Here exists his transcendence, his leaping beyond History and the world of normal men who seek to create themselves in doing and making. But there is no leaping out of History or refuting the evil of time; time and History mock Ch'en's efforts. We see Malraux's symbolism underscoring Ch'en's unequal combat with destiny. The revolutionaries are gathered in a clock shop, and while Ch'en mutters that politics is mere talk and that only killing Chiang matters, ". . . all the pendulums and balance wheels of the various time-pieces . . . went on ticking their measure." Ch'en's acts, in the current radical jargon, are counterproductive; they irritate the Dialectic in ways inimical to the revolutionary cause. The arms made available through Ch'en's initial murder are surrendered to the Kuomintang and subsequently used against the Communists. Ch'en's blundered attempt on Chiang's life goes unnoticed and his gesture of self-destruction never achieves the status of a martyr's act. Fooled by History, Ch'en lives and dies unremembered by history.

3

Men like Ch'en, tormented by apocalyptic yearnings, cannot be dismissed as merely unfortunate by-products of revolutionary crisis. Those struggling in the very midst of events begin to see the Revolution not in its ultimate eschatological aspects, as history working toward social justice and human happiness, but as The End Itself. They become obsessed with Revolution as a sufficient activity, a way of life which justifies itself. The Revolution, rather than being a means toward a desirable historical goal, becomes the present in which History achieves its apotheosis. Garcia, the Communist intellectual in *Man's Hope,* warns against substituting revolutionary fervor and the heady exhilarations of ideological excitement for the military and organizational efficiency which wins wars:

"The apocalyptic mood clamours for everything right away. Tenacity of purpose wins through bit by bit; slowly, laboriously. That apocalyptic fervour is ingrained in every one of us; and there's the danger. For that fervour spells certain defeat, after a relatively short period, and for a very simple reason: it's in the very nature of an apocalypse to have no future. . . . Even when it professes to have one."

Putting his pipe back in his pocket, he added sadly: "Our humble task, Monsieur Magnin, is to *organize* the apocalypse."

"To *organize* the apocalypse . . ." Paradoxes can be fructifying, functioning as creative centers in literary work. *Organized apocalypse* might conceivably define the successful work of art where inchoate elements of raw experience are ordered into significance by ethical and structural control. But *Man's Hope,* Malraux's full-scale attempt to render the historical immediacy of the Spanish Civil War, strikes me as a disorganized apocalypse. It is Malraux's most ambitious fictional work, Tolstoyean in its sprawling proportions and ideological scope. Apparently Malraux tried to tell us everything he observed, everything he felt, everything he *did* (for he was part of the action) in Spain. Malraux also intended the book to speak for the Loyalist cause; it was meant to influence the course of history in a way fervently desired by men and women opposed to fascism. Unfortunately, *Man's Hope* is disappointing as a novel and largely unconvincing as a work of special pleading.

Partisanship need not in itself violate the integrity of a novel. Most readers share Malraux's partisanship; most of Malraux's admirers (including myself) came to political consciousness and made their first overt political affirmations during the Spanish Civil War. But Malraux's ideological commitment expresses itself in tedious sermonizing—in blatantly hollow rationalizations for Communist "efficiency" and for a

soldierly discipline which must be inculcated by terror. Conse-
quently, Malraux's didactic passages detach themselves from
the fictional process. In *Man's Fate* the claims of ideology
issue from the clash of character and the developing action; in
Man's Hope the action is too confused and the characters too
briefly glimpsed to develop more than a cartoon ideology of
slogans. Formalist literary theory points out that propaganda
makes for bad art; *Man's Hope* shows that bad art makes for
ineffective propaganda.

Malraux was in indecent haste to record history as it was
happening. The Spanish Civil War broke out in July 1936;
Man's Hope was completed in the last month of 1937 and
published early in 1938. The book ends with the Loyalist victory at Teruel (December 19, 1937)—a heartbreakingly brief
triumph, for Teruel was recaptured by Franco in February
1938. *Man's Hope* moves with history as it happened, a book
so close to events that it develops a coy attitude of busy self-
consciousness. It is filled with what William Empson calls
"the hearty revolutionary romp," an embarrassing sentimen-
tality about comradeship in arms couched in stiffly unreal
dialogue. The largest self-consciousness is the constant awareness which the characters express about their roles in the drama
of History; here is Colonel Ximenes addressing his men:

> "Listen my lads," he said, "we've taken that farm. The
> men who disobeyed orders and left cover are dismissed
> from the column, whether they reached the farm or not.
> Don't forget that we're under observation. History is
> watching us, is judging and will judge us, and it calls for
> the sort of courage that goes in and wins, not the courage
> that consoles. . . ."

This is a speech ostensibly delivered during the heat of actual
battle. Its falseness is not a matter of "verisimilitude": of
whether such oratory might not have been actually delivered.
The words may have been transcribed from Malraux's note-
book. But neither Colonel Ximenes's exhortations to his men
nor dozens of other similar passages of political argumenta-
tion, ideological posturings, and intellectual debate ever
achieve that sufficiency of style which carries the language and
rhythm of utter conviction.

Immersed in action and event *Man's Hope* never develops functioning protagonists—characters who speak and act for themselves, out of individual will and inner struggle. Manuel the Good Soldier and Garcia the Wise Political Commissar, whom we see more than other characters and whom we might consider the heroes of the book, never seem more than the articulations of ideology. No characters emerge like Kyo who balances in a precarious and very human tension the demands of personal wish and political idealism; like Old Gisors in whom we see a man holding passionate attachments yet living and recommending a life of non-attachment; like Ferral in whom we see a man claiming to create his own nature and destiny yet humiliated by his obsessive erotomania and tricked by the unexpected turn of events. Of the major characters who force themselves on the reader's imagination, one, Captain Hernandez, remains wholly memorable. A sensitive and generous nature, he is captured by the fascists and condemned to death. Although convinced of the justice of the Loyalist position, Hernandez is tormented by what he feels to be a growing disparity between means and ends and between his own very high sense of personal honor and dignity and the practical necessities of the battlefield. He realizes that the war can be won only by abrogating the moral code by which he has lived and *for* which he has joined the Loyalist side. Unlike the Communists, sustained by the faith that a successful Revolution resolves the contradictions necessary to its making, he is sickened by the costs of action. Torn by doubts, disillusioned, Hernandez faces the fascist firing squad with heroic indifference.

The scene of Hernandez's execution (the most vivid and moving in *Man's Hope*) affords two authorial observations on History. In the first Malraux seems to assert the primacy of the moment, the triviality of the past before the intolerable fact that men will die, *will cease to be human creatures:*

> Three fascists had just led off three prisoners and, after posting them on the edge of the ditch, had withdrawn.
> "Ready!"
> The condemned man on the left had a mop of round-cropped hair. The three men were posted on a ridge

above the level of the watching group, and stood out, taller than life, against the historic mountain-range beyond the Tagus. But how small a thing is history beside living—still living—flesh and blood!

The second observation on History mildly rebukes Hernandez for his aristocratic code of honor; it is also tinged with punitive irony as Malraux explains that History is "made" with blood and tears:

> Bright air shimmered on the Tagus hills and bathed Toledo in a crystal sheen. Hernandez was beginning to learn how history is made. Once more in this land of black-clothed women, as so often in the past, a generation of widows was in the making. When such things are being done, what is the meaning of "nobility?" Or "generosity?"
>
> Hernandez felt his eyes yearning towards the fresh-turned earth. Earth, inert, reposeful . . . Only living men are torn by anguish and disgust.

Hernandez pits strength and courage, the moral force of his will against the powers of History and loses. He flunks the test of action.

Later in *Man's Hope* Garcia argues eloquently against those who refuse to take sides or who succumb to metaphysical despair about the moral ambiguities of action. The "great intellectual" mentioned in the following passage is Miguel de Unamuno, who had briefly sided with Franco but then later repudiated his partisanship:

> The great intellectual is a man of subtleties, of fine shades, of evaluations; he's interested in absolute truth and in the complexity of things. He is—how shall I put it?— "antimanichean" by definition, by nature. But all forms of action are manichean, because all action pays a tribute to the devil; that manichean element is most intense when the masses are involved. Every true revolutionary is a born manichean. The same is true of politics, all politics.

Garcia shows an intellectual's sensitivity to the dilemma of the intellectual when faced with making absolute political choices, or the dilemma of a man like Hernandez who turns ". . . in his sad small orbit of despair like a madman turning in his cell." But Garcia speaks with a forked tongue. He is capable of making difficult and delicate distinctions: of recognizing that only in action can politics become an effective means of bettering the conditions in which men live, and at the same time recognizing that action stains with a deep and indelible moral taint. He also talks that queer mixture of platitude and arrogant self-justification which was heard from the apologists for Stalinism during the period from the Moscow trials to the Stalin-Hitler pact of August 1939.

Perhaps the confusions and contradictions of *Man's Hope* can best be glimpsed in the way Malraux treats Hernandez and Garcia. Garcia extols action and organization and the virtues of an efficient military machine. Garcia, however, only talks; it is Hernandez whom we see acting. We remember Garcia only as the Communist intellectual, a mouthpiece for Malraux's ideological preferences. We remember Hernandez as the hero of two magnificent episodes, rendered with all the art Malraux owns: the generous and compassionate man before the Alcazar, and the courageous, almost otherworldly victim of the fascist firing squad. Finally, in his zeal to justify his views, Garcia patronizes Hernandez and the psychological debilities which led to his death.

Malraux thus reveals a deep discrepancy between "showing" and "telling." We are told that action is preferable to contemplation; the man who tells us this is an intellectual. We are shown the contemplative man Hernandez in action; he is not an intellectual but a professional soldier. Malraux lavishes some of the finest writing in the book on the episode of Hernandez's execution. It would seem, then, that Malraux's political self prefers Garcia, the intellectual who talks about action but does not act; that Malraux's artistic self prefers Hernandez the soldier who acts and dies despairing of the efficacy of action. Malraux is not unaware that ideology and reality are unbalanced in *Man's Hope* and that the political and propagandistic elements require dialectical correction. Alvear the art historian speaks for Malraux the cultivated humanist, the Malraux of *The Walnut Trees of Altenburg* and the gorgeously illustrated art books. Alvear excoriates politics and the loss of civility and decency occasioned by the revolution; he only hopes that the fighting will not destroy "The human element; the quality of man."

Malraux took too many risks in *Man's Hope*. He assumed the stability, humanity, and efficiency of the Communist leadership. He tried to outguess History or perhaps outshout it. Throughout *Man's Hope* Malraux makes it abundantly clear that Franco has every military advantage; yet Malraux ends the book on a note of hope, the brief (as it turned out) Loyalist victory at Teruel. He largely forsook the structural conventions of plot and character and tried to create a fictional world out of episodes, tones, moods, and pages of brilliant writing. He tried to write a book about a political conflict from a partisan stance and hoped the book itself would become part of the action and help summon the democratic world to the aid of Loyalist Spain. Parts of *Man's Hope* struggle free of its ideological and structural shackles; but a book so conceived and written was doomed as was the cause it so desperately espoused.

4

Malraux's career as a novelist is framed by two works, *The Temptation of the West* (1926) and *The Walnut Trees of Altenburg* (1943). Although he has been busy since the end of World War II as a writer on art and has published his *Anti-Memoirs,* Malraux has ceased writing novels. These two books, then, represent a beginning and an end. Not surprisingly, they echo each other's concerns although they diverge in structure and *genre. The Temptation of the West* is an exchange of letters between a young Chinese, Ling-W.-Y. and a young Frenchman, A.D. There is no narrative and only the faintest delineation of individual character; this short book consists largely of passages of fine writing alternating with aperçus on culture and History, and on what Karl Mannheim calls "the interpretation of *Weltanschauung.*" The opening section might be a passage from the *Anabase* of St.-J. Perse:

> In the center of the square, evil magicians are being burned at an odoriferous stake; the figurines of hollow

wood, which they had used to cast spells on princesses, explode and shoot up like fireworks. The crowd—so many blind men!—falls back quickly. Near the horizon, in the wild grass, a line of ant-covered bones marks the path of armies. Not far from the fire, the magicians' widows have seen the future.

The main thrust of *The Temptation of the West,* with its extreme cultural relativism and its anti-rational historicism, is Spenglerian. A.D. and Ling represent those self-contained and coherent entities of West and East; their thoughts and feelings are meant as expressions of their respective cultures, or in Spenglerian capitals, Cultures. Malraux is a more re-fined thinker than Spengler; he has a certain delicacy in mak-ing distinctions, a greater sensitivity to moral questions, and a less heavy-handed, less offensively self-assured way of making generalizations. Despite differences of tone and style, and, of course, scope, *The Temptation of the West* and *The Decline of the West* urge a set of similar theses. Essentially the West— by which Malraux and Spengler designate "West-European-American" culture—is committed to time and history. The Faustian ideals of Europe emphasize personality, individuality, achievement, goals. Men seek themselves in action, in those struggles which "make history"; and they seek this self-fulfill-ment with fevered intellectual awareness. Like Nietzsche Malraux questions a culture that exalts intellect over life and increasingly removes itself from nature. Ling notes that while men of the East are satisfied to let the world change them, men of the West are perennially engaged in changing the world. In the East men seek to hear the rhythms of the cosmos and live contentedly to a serene music; in the West men im-pose the form and shape of their ego upon the world: so that the world becomes, in Spengler's phrase, "the world-as-history." Ling summarizes the differences he sees between East and West:

> Between Western and Eastern intellect I sense above all a difference of direction, almost of aim. The former desires to construct a plan of the universe and give it an intelligible form; that is, to establish between the unknown and the known a relation capable of bringing to light things which have been obscure. It wants to

subordinate the universe, and finds in this desire a pride that becomes greater the more intellect seems to dominate the universe. Its cosmos is a coherent myth. The Eastern mind, on the other hand, gives no value to man himself; it contrives to find, in the flow of the universe, the thoughts which permit it to break its human bonds. The first wants to bring the universe to man; the second offers man up to the universe. . . .

Ling's views derive more from Nietzsche than from the inscrutable Wisdom of the East. His critique of knowledge, of the European itch to analyze and systematize, rehearses the charges Nietzsche leveled against European civilization. A.D. expands the argument and points out that European achievements in art and historical research increase rather than alleviate the sickness of knowing. Modern art develops its own private symbolism which ". . . can be 'learned' like a foreign language . . ."; but the succession of novelties in painting, poetry, and music becomes ". . . an agonizing force which dominates the mind. The continual attempt to renew certain aspects of the universe by looking at them with new eyes is an effort involving an ardent ingenuity, which acts on man like a drug." The effort to understand the past also grows burdensome; and in the West the past is preserved in museums and libraries, in the evocative splendor of formal gardens and the oppressive grandeur of monumental architecture. Everywhere Western man looks, as he walks in his immense cities, he discovers his past and his own agonized, power driven soul. Western man hopes to find salvation in his own history; he belongs to ". . . a race which, in order to regain its greatest thoughts, only knows how to entreat its unfaithful dead. . . ."

Of course, his search only exacerbates and increases his illness, his unchecked drive toward intellectual domination of his universe. Malraux echoes Gerontion's exhortation on History, especially those lines figuring knowledge as sexual appetite which grows all the more insatiable when satisfied:

> *Think now*
> *She gives when our attention is distracted.*
> *And what she gives, gives with such supple confusions*
> *That the giving famishes the craving.*

Western and Eastern attitudes toward love and eroticism figure similarly in *The Temptation of the West*. Ling notes that Western self-consciousness and will-to-power, the Western mode of conceiving time and history, also dominate Western ideas of love and attitudes toward women. Ling expresses puzzlement at the fact that Western man takes woman seriously, that he attempts to "understand" her and to regard her as a unique individual. "Men and women belong to different species." Ling's meditation on the Western erotic sensibility leads to this italicized insight: *at the core of European man, ruling the important movements of his life, is a basic absurdity.*

The Absurd fills the vacant space once occupied by the divine presence. Man has learned that he himself created the gods; such knowledge earns no forgiveness for the men who promulgate it. Nor does modern civilization function as an adequate surrogate for the loss of the sacred and its ordering of action and morality. Man sacrifices himself in his institutions and his cultural achievements; A.D. writes, "At the core of Western civilization there is a hopeless contradiction, in whatever shape we discover it: that between man and what he has created. . . . Sweeping away facts and, finally, itself, this spirit of contradiction trains our consciousness to give way and prepares us for the metallic realms of the absurd." What Malraux seems to be saying (the tone of *The Temptation of the West* wavers between absolute assertion and hesitant denial) is that the contradiction contradicts itself; again we hear Hegelian overtones—although whatever Hegel Malraux absorbed probably came through his reading of Nietzsche and Spengler. In both substance and method Malraux formulates Hegel's theory of alienation: that man sacrifices himself in culture and becomes spiritually estranged from the objective world he constructs. To overcome the absurd and retrieve his self from alienation, Western man joins ". . . a race subject to the test of action, and thus destined to a most bloody fate."

Action, blood, and fate stand as rubrics on every page of Malraux's novels. While some have called Malraux's espousal of revolutionary causes instances of political opportunism or adventurism, his commitment to action hurled a challenge across "the metallic realms of the absurd." To be sure, Malraux was afflicted with that *amor fati* which in Spengler means submitting to historical necessity and those historical forces poised to destroy man's freedom and man himself. Spengler's peroration to the second volume of *The Decline of the West* urges men to join with ". . . the Caesarism that approaches quietly and irresistibly. . . ." In a phrase recalling Engels ("Freedom is the recognition of necessity") Spengler issues the orders of the day, "We do not have the freedom to attain this or that, but the freedom to do the necessary or nothing. And a problem posed by historical necessity will be solved with the individual or *in spite of him*." Spengler concludes his philosophy of history with this menacing line from the *Aeneid:*

Ducunt fata volentem, nolentem trahunt

"The fates lead the willing, drag the unwilling."[6]

5

Even though early in his career Malraux urged the refutation of Spengler, he was obviously caught up in his ideas. Malraux accepted the fatality of History and Spengler's closed, organic view of culture. Every culture had its spring, summer, autumn, and winter; no culture can escape its final dissolution any more than man can resist the change of seasons. Man as an individual, then, is the helpless victim of historical process. Spengler's view of history derives from "a crude half-baked, subjective idealism"[7] which sees every man trapped within the circle of his own perceptions; communication outside the circle is impossible. By a slippery analogy *The Decline of the West* asserts that every great culture stands isolated in a closed circle whose circumference touches no other culture and whose center is the controlling *Schicksalsidee*.

In *The Walnut Trees of Altenburg* Malraux introduces a character, the German ethnologist Möllberg, who advances Spengler's basic assumptions. He discourses with a group of intellectuals in the great library at Altenburg; this discourse occupies a central position in the book: an essay on the meaning of history which stands between the two immense historical actions of the West in the twentieth century, the

First and Second World Wars. The book falls into three precisely delineated periods of time. The first part, *Chartres Camp,* takes place in Chartres cathedral which has been turned into a prisoner-of-war camp; the time is June 1940, immediately after the French defeat. The second part, which includes the discussion at Altenburg, takes place during the years 1908–1915; the protagonist of the second part is Vincent Berger, father of the Berger who narrates the first and final sections. The third section takes place before the opening scenes in Chartres, when French armored units are going into action against the invading Germans. Berger commands a tank and he views his world from inside the isolation of his machine, a private ego searching the landscape of events.

Despite *The Walnut Trees of Altenburg*'s heavy involvements with the two world wars, it is the least public of Malraux's books. It is also the least parochial, without political or ideological stridencies. The first and third parts, the enclosing sections, show Berger as a soldier fighting against the Germans; in the important middle section the elder Berger fights with the German army on the Eastern Front. The Bergers belong to an Alsatian family and their national attachments are German during the First World War, French during the Second. This international note is deliberate and purely fictional; Malraux remarks in the *Anti-Memoirs,* "I knew nothing of Alsace. . . . The family is called Berger because this name can be either French or German according to pronunciation."[8] Not that *The Walnut Trees of Altenburg* avoids autobiographical episodes; Malraux depicts certain members of his family and, in slight disguises, episodes from his own career. He would insist, however, that these episodes serve a larger meaning, the total pattern of incidents which form the thematic concern of the book. And because of the peculiar way that life has of imitating art, certain fictional scenes prove prophetic. "Often linked to memory by inextricable bonds, they sometimes turn out, more disturbingly, to be linked to the future too."[9]

A number of texts have figured crucially in this study. Henry Adams's chapter on History as the Dynamo, Gerontion's negative appeal to History, and Yeats's myth of recurrence all make explicit a complex of theories about the meaning of history. The discussion in the library at Altenburg belongs among these crucial texts. Walter Berger, uncle to Vincent Berger and great-uncle to the narrator of the first and third sections, had established these "Altenburg Conferences." Every year Walter Berger invited to Altenburg a distinguished group of intellectuals to present papers and engage in discussions on large questions: ". . . he gathered there some of his more eminent colleagues, intellectuals from various countries, and the most gifted of his former pupils. Papers by Max Weber, Stefan George, Sorel, Durkheim, and Freud were born of these discussions." Walter asks Vincent to attend a session at Altenburg; ". . . the theme of the conference . . . was the permanence of man through the rise and fall of civilizations."

Möllberg, the German ethnologist, is the principal speaker. Malraux heavily emphasizes the Germanic qualities of Möllberg's approach and the fact that Germany had provided modern European thought with its concept of historical destiny. "[Möllberg's] system . . . was the officially recognized German approach to the problems of history; and ever since Hegel Germany in her role of revealer of man's destiny has received violent, impassioned recognition." With all the authority of his scholarship and his dominating, almost terrifying personality, Möllberg pushes his thesis. Drawing his evidence from primitive societies who live bound to the cosmos and nature, he sees all mankind ". . . thoroughly defined and classified by their form of fatalism. . . ." As certain proto-historical cultures were bound to the phases of the moon and the position of the stars, modern man is linked to the historical realm. "We live in it, as the religious civilization lived in God. Without it, not one of us—I merely say: 'not one'— would be able to think. It's our only realm: it's history." Like Spengler, Möllberg insists each culture it utterly permeated by a mental structure which has no basis in rationality but which ". . . is to man what the aquarium is to the fish swimming inside it." When this mental structure decays or disappears, man dies. The full flavor of German historical pessimism can be savored in Möllberg's bitter epitaph for humanity:

"But perhaps these mental structures disappear without a trace like the dinosaur; perhaps civilizations must go on succeeding one another only to cast man into the bottomless pit of nothingness; perhaps the human adventure can only be sustained at the price of a relentless process of metamorphosis. In which case, it matters little that men hand down to one another their concepts and their techniques for a few centuries: for man is an accident, and the world, essentially, is made of oblivion."

He shrugged his shoulders and repeated, like an echo, "Oblivion . . ."

Because Möllberg overwhelms the gathering at Altenburg with the length and intensity of his remarks, it has seemed to many critics his arguments simply demolish the humanist ideal that man has permanent and valuable qualities and the belief that a concept of man transcends his fatal attachments to nature and history. Malraux accepts in *The Temptation of the West* Spengler's vision of a Western culture committed to a bloody dynamism, an escalation of historical action culminating in a crisis of civilization. But Malraux rejects the ultimate term of Möllberg's Spenglerian argument, the final extinction of man and man's work in culture. He refutes Möllberg's thesis in three separate sorties of dialectic: first, in the objections raised at the Altenburg conference; second, in Möllberg's own arguments which cannot withstand factual and logical scrutiny; and third and most important, in the structure of *The Walnut Trees of Altenburg*. We need hardly stress that an author's beliefs are more accurately communicated through his narrative and his symbols than through what individual characters say.

We cannot, however, discount what the characters say. The discussion at Altenburg reaches out thematic lines which run through the book and through Malraux's series of critical works on the plastic arts. One of the presiding spirits at the discussion is Nietzsche. He is not physically present but his radical humanism has inspired the thinking of both Walter and Vincent Berger. The narrator, Berger *fils,* observes, "My father loved Nietzsche more than any other writer. Not for

what he preached but for the incomparable generosity of spirit
which he found in him." Now the Möllberg-Spengler thesis
completely lacks spiritual generosity; it is the dark and narrow formulation of a vindictive intelligence. Walter, drawing
on the Nietzschean vision of a world apprehended and justified
by the aesthetic sensibility, affirms man's continued existence in
the works of art which he draws from within himself:

> The greatest mystery is not that we have been flung
> at random between the profusion of matter and of the
> stars, but that within this prison we can draw from our-
> selves images powerful enough to deny our nothingness.

Art sends a ray of light down the corridor of history; and the
meaning of history need not depend solely on the ethically
ambiguous outcome of human action. The affirmation of man's
immortality through art does not, of course, originate with
Nietzsche. It was already a commonplace of Renaissance
thought when Shakespeare, with self-assured confidence in his
own genius, explains to the young man of the sonnets that he
is being singled out for immortality.

Other members of the Altenburg group challenge Möllberg's anti-humanist pessimism. Count Rabaud articulates a
familiar Malraux idea, that man's ability to interrogate the
world, in either art or action, links him to a principle which
opposes his historical destiny. "Something eternal lives in
man—in thinking man—something that I shall call his divine
quality: it's his ability to call the world in question." The
philosopher, the saint, the prophet all bring the world under
scrutiny; their passions and thoughts not only interpret but
transform the world. Möllberg sourly counters that the work
of the spirit cannot be transmitted from one culture to another.
Contacts between different cultures are violent encounters:
"Plato and St. Paul can neither agree with each other nor convince each other: they can only convert each other." This is
Spenglerism *in extremis,* a superb example of how Spengler
loads the dice by refusing to examine those facts of history
which do not suit his theory. The agreement between Plato
and Paul, between classical philosophy and Christian theology,
is, from one point of view, *the* history of Western thought from

Augustine to Aquinas and from Aquinas to the Christian humanism of the Renaissance.

At least one member of the Altenburg group, Stieglitz, applauds Möllberg's performance. He sees it in the Hegelian tradition, a culmination of nineteenth century German historical and philosophical thought. "The great line of Hegelianism remains intact. The point at issue is the integration in the *Weltgeist* of the facts acquired through our new knowledge, etc. . . ." Spengler saw himself in the line of Hegel and Nietzsche, invoking them both in the concluding paragraph to *The Decline of the West*. But Spengler only adopts aspects of Hegel's methodology, and either imitates Nietzsche's thunder and lightning rhetoric or simply plagiarizes from him. (Compare, for example, the opening of the second volume of *The Decline of the West*, "The Cosmic and the Microcosm," with the opening of Nietzsche's "Of the Use and Disadvantage of History.") Where Hegel sees in history continuity, synthesis, mediation, the expansion of human freedom, Spengler sees isolation, fragmentation, conflict, the decay of individual rights. Where Nietzsche urges man to live intensely in the present and free himself from the historical process, Spengler tells man he must join the militarists who are planning his destruction. Nietzsche's *amor fati* is heroic, Spengler's is cringing.

The movement of ideas, the shift of metaphysical counters at the conference at Altenburg precede accounts of two apocalyptic actions. In the first Berger *père* participates in a gas attack launched by the Germans against the Russians; in the second Berger *fils* escapes death from the bottom of a tank trap. Malraux's irony is clear; after listening to abstract talk about History, about the problems of Culture and Cosmos and *Weltgeist,* we plunge into actual history: human suffering and death. Both episodes emphasize that the antagonist of man is not the fatalism of history or the inexorable decay of nature but man's inhumanity to himself. The gas attack reaches such an unbearable level of horror that the German soldiers throw away their rifles and attempt to rescue the gagging, scorched Russians. Vincent Berger forgets his nationality and his duty as an officer; he is in the presence of absolute evil. "The Spirit of Evil was stronger here than death, so strong that he felt compelled to find a Russian, any Russian who had not been killed, put him on his shoulders and save him." The German soldiers, each with a gassed Russian on his back, advance through the hellishly devastated landscape. No scene in Malraux engenders such feelings of overpowering terror and compassion; so much that the irruption of radical evil followed by transcendent good becomes understandable only in religious terms. The attempt of the Germans to rescue their enemies is a redemptive act; in the midst of action, and, at least for the moment, time and history are filled with meaning—with the human charity St. Paul urges upon mankind and without which speech and action are as sounding brass.

The gas attack on the Eastern Front in the First World War is an apocalypse *organized* and redeemed by the purely human. Such an apocalypse cannot be the end of time, the ordained *eschaton* with its trumpet music, cracking open of graves, and final judgment. Like Eliot in the *Quartets,* Malraux sees the disturbances of modern history as recurrent apocalypses; the literary imagination nurtured on crisis sees the end in every moment. Such a view, suffused with pathos and dread, allows a modicum of hope. The second Doomsday episode in *The Walnut Trees of Altenburg* stands as an analogue to the gas attack. The time is now the Second World War; the narrator is Berger *fils* in command of a French tank hurrying to meet the invading Germans. "Suddenly every nearby shape disappeared, except for the treetops; at ground level nothing was visible; our accompanying tanks were enveloped in darkness. A cloud must have blotted out the moon. . . ." Berger and his crew are cut off from the other tanks, from the upper world itself as "sucked in by the earth" they careen into a tank trap. Through hysterical effort and miraculous accident—though targeted by German shellfire they are never hit—they finally escape from "the sepulcher of the pit." They spend the night in a farming village; and to Berger the following "morning was as pure as if the war did not exist."

The sense of survival and its attendant feelings of elation, relief, and gratitude suffuse the final episode of *The Walnut*

Trees of Altenburg. The murderous encounters of men and machines, even the harrowing experience of the previous night, yield to Berger's sense of rebirth. Simple objects like watering cans and brooms are transfigured into symbols; nature once again seems capable of the fabulous. Berger's sensibility invests every object and every feature of the world with mythic implications. Life is very old and very new. An ancient peasant couple, also survivors from time's abyss, sit quietly in the sun, "Attuned to the cosmos like a stone." Berger reflects:

> I knew now the meaning of the ancient myths about the living being snatched from the dead. I scarcely remembered death; what I bore within me was the discovery of a very simple secret, incommunicable and sacred.
>
> Thus it was, perhaps, that God looked at the first man.

The Walnut Trees of Altenburg ends on the morning of man's first day. Mankind, if not eternally redeemed from the merciless process of disintegration prophesied by Möllberg, is granted a blessed reprieve.

Berger inhabits Nietzsche's sun-filled "mid-day of life."[10] Here, in an ongoing present, the world seems redeemed from the disorders and agonies of History. Time pauses while Berger hesitates between past and future, the nightmares of action. He forgets the terrors of the night; they no longer exist. This step out of time and history is a descent into Zarathustra's "well of eternity." Berger "overcomes" history as Zarathustra overcomes the despair of living in a world emptied of God. Malraux proposes no "solution" to the problem of history; he shifts from his emphasis on the struggle between will and destiny, and shows us man with a relaxed will released from the imperatives of his fate. Like the traditional man of the East described by Ling, Berger is content, *at that moment,* to allow the universe to shape his fate. He exists— Adam in the Garden—before the tragic history of the West begins.

Malraux, however, does not cop out. The finale of *The Walnut Trees of Altenburg* hardly repudiates the achievement of Malraux's previous work and its relentless inquiry into the nature of historical process. Rather, in turning away from the dynamics of struggle to an image of a-historic man, Malraux brings us back to "The human element; the quality of man." Those who undergo or inflict the tests of action play a role of high excitement; they "make," think they make, or are made by History. But the quality of man was there in the beginning and will survive after the end.

> *And the end and the beginning were always there*
> *Before the beginning and after the end.*

VII
Thomas Mann

> ... the concept of signaling is of the foremost importance
> in all literature and all study of literature. That the writer
> (and the philosopher also) is a reporting instrument, seis-
> mograph, medium of sensitivity, though lacking clear
> knowledge of his organic function and therefore quite cap-
> able of wrong judgments also—this seems to me the only
> proper perspective on writing.
>
> —Thomas Mann, *The Story of a Novel*

I

Mann's earliest work is sealed off from the grosser incursions
of History. The brilliantly executed stories of cripples, out-
siders, and dilettantes breathe heavily the moist air of late
nineteenth-century *Weltschmerz*. But they wear their decadence with a difference; the deformity of Little Herr Friede-
mann and the boredom of The Bajazzo suggest, if ever so
quietly, the symptoms of a general disorder. After the publication of *Buddenbrooks* (1901) we see an intensified awareness
of "the cultural situation": not directly in politics but indi-
rectly in that clash of ideas engendered by Mann's understanding of the equivocal relationship between literature and living,
art and morals, nature and spirit. We need not multiply the
polarities; any careful reader of Mann knows he is the wizard
of the dialectical double-whammy, the crafty Wotan of position and counter-position.

In those remarkable stories, beginning with "Gladius Dei"
(1902) and culminating with *Death in Venice* (1911–12), there

appear a series of signal men—prophets if you will—who flash the message that European civilization was built over a fault and that the earthquake, the tidal wave, and the fire were imminent. Now a writer is only a prophet after the fact, and our naming Mann a prophet (more exactly, the ironical creator of prophets) is a matter of hindsight, ours as critic and Mann's as a lavish commentator on his own work. Like Eliot, Mann distrusted "the backward devils" and placed between himself and his prophetic characters a complex structure of attitudes, a long and richly detailed foreground of ambivalence, ironic detachment, and fascinated involvement.

The short sketch "At the Prophet's" (1904) states some basic thematic material typifying Mann's concern with prophecy and its questionable ramifications. Our protagonist is Mann him self, identified as "The novelist, a gentleman with a stiff hat and a well-cared-for moustache . . . He was on good terms with life: a book of his was read in middle-class circles." (The book was *Buddenbrooks,* then enjoying a considerable critical and financial success.) He attends a reading at the apartment of one Daniel, the leader of a hermetic cult whose doctrine combines in an unwholesome mixture a rarefied aestheticism and a ferocious dedication to violence. Daniel does not appear but one of his younger disciples reads from his "Proclamations."

> The "Proclamations" consisted of sermons, parables, theses, laws, prophecies, and exhortations resembling orders of the day, following each other in a mingled style of psalter and revelation with an endless succession of technical phrases, military and strategic as well as philosophical and critical. A fevered and frightfully irritable ego here expanded itself, a self-isolated megalomaniac flooded the world with a hurricane of violent and threatening words. *Christus imperator maximus* was his name; he enrolled troops ready to die for the subjection of the globe; he sent out embassies, gave inexorable ultimata, exacted poverty and chastity, and with a sort of morbid enjoyment reiterated his roaring demand for unconditional obedience. Buddha, Alexander, Napoleon and Jesus—their names were mentioned as his humble forerunners, not worthy to unloose the laces of their spiritual lord. . . . The solitary ego sang, raved, commanded. It would lose itself

in confused pictures, go down in an eddy of logical error, to bob up again suddenly and startlingly in an entirely unexpected place. Blasphemies and hosannahs—a waft of incense and a reek of blood. In thunderings and slaughterings the world was conquered and redeemed.[1]

The novelist's attitude during this performance is attentive, if somewhat strained and less than completely respectful. "The novelist searched vainly for a comfortable position for his aching back. At ten o'clock there came a vision of a ham sandwich, but he manfully banished it." Immediately following this mundane visitation comes the apocalyptic conclusion to the "Proclamations": "At about half past ten one saw that the young man held the last folio sheet in his red, trembling hand. He had reached the end. 'Soldiers,' he concluded, at the very limit of his strength and with his thundering voice failing, 'I hand over to you for plundering—*the world!*' "

Mann's reaction to this unseemly rhetorical display and to the motley audience—which includes "a philosopher with the face of a kangaroo" and a female adept of Eros—and to the shabby Bohemian surroundings is amused contempt and unwilling fascination. As an artist he recognizes that Daniel possesses at least some attributes of poetic genius; he also recognizes those elements which bring the artist close to criminality and madness. What he sees in Daniel is the distorted image of himself; in every artist lurks the Bohemian, the madman, even the criminal. We recall that Tonio Kröger was mistaken for a shady character in his own home town.

Mann does not leave it a simple matter of rejecting the extremism of Daniel and congratulating himself on his bourgeois levelheadedness and moral stability. He pokes gentle fun at himself—for those very middle-class virtues which sustain his air of detachment and condescension. At the conclusion of the story, he deferentially greets an elegantly turned out wealthy woman—deliberately modeled on his future mother-in-law, Frau Professor Hedwig Pringsheim.[2] He sends greetings to her daughter, his fiancée, and refers to her familiarly by her first name. "He looked anxiously into her face to see how she would respond that he spoke simply of 'Sonia,' not 'Miss Sonia' or 'your daughter.' " Our novelist minds his manners; he also notes in his manners a touch of subservience, a touch of priggishness. But these are the failings of common humanity. The failings of the prophet Daniel—arrogance, violence, contempt for life—are untouched by humanity or love. At the conclusion of "At the Prophet's," the novelist, "hungry as a wolf" for his supper, declares that he and life are on excellent terms. Again, this declaration is tempered by ironic self-deprecation: by the feeling that such a declaration is touched by smugness.

Forty years later Mann returned to the prophet Daniel. He appears again in *Doctor Faustus* as the poet Daniel zur Höhe; his descriptive cognomen is taken from a phrase in "At the Prophet's," "*aus höchster Höhe, aus Daniels Reich*—from the highest heights, from Daniel's domain." Daniel zur Höhe belongs to a group of artists and scholars who meet at the Munich home of Sextus Kridwiss. (Mann later identified zur Höhe as Ludwig Derleth, a minor poet and apostate follower of Stefan George.)[3] Mann's resurrection of Daniel is an act of deliberate cultural and political criticism. The poet-prophet and the so-called "Kridwiss circle" speculate on the infamous order of ideas which first made their appearance in Daniel's "Proclamations." In "At the Prophet's" Mann smelled the morally noxious elements in the "Proclamations": the mixture of violence and extravagant metaphor, of fraudulent religiosity and brutal military fervor. In *Doctor Faustus,* Mann, in his guise of the humanist Serenus Zeitblom, finds Daniel's prophecies "the boldest aesthetic misdemeanor" he has ever encountered; he sees in them the seeds of a dangerous new politics.

The "Kridwiss circle" raises Daniel's "Proclamations"— the work of a demented aesthete influenced by prevailing fashions in decadence and the more unrestrained pronouncements of Nietzsche—to the level of desirable political necessities. They discuss the coming of a new order which shall sacrifice the individual to the community, glorify violence over intellect and scientific knowledge, and establish the power of blood, soil, and myth over the enfeebled European tradition of reason and democratic institutions. The men of the Kridwiss circle are the new "doctrinaires of the irrational"[4] and their new order

> . . . an old-new world of revolutionary reaction, in which the values bound up with the idea of the individual—shall we say truth, freedom, law, reason?—were entirely rejected and shorn of power, or else had taken on a meaning quite different from that given them for centuries. Wrenched away from the washed-out theoretic, based on the relative and pumped full of fresh blood, they were referred to the far higher court of violence, authority, the dictatorship of belief—not, let me say, in a reactionary, anachronistic way as of yesterday or the day before, but so that it was like the most novel setting back of humanity into mediaevally theocratic conditions and situations. That was as little reactionary as though one were to describe as regression the track round a sphere, which of course leads back to where it started. There it was: progress and reaction, the old and the new, the past and the future became one; the political Right more and more coincided with the Left.[5]

Zeitblom complains that not only did the gentlemen of the Kridwiss circle sense the catastrophes to come, they also, like Yeats's Magi, profoundly desired them. They longed for the bloodshed, the abyss, the apocalypse. Zeitblom points out that their ability to prophesy the new barbarism derived from a profound and perverse sympathy with it. Their insights were not delivered in sorrow and anger, as fruits from the wrath-bearing tree, but in a spirit of frivolous identification and delighted anticipation. They betrayed the high office of prophecy which must cry out against evil and moral disaster: ". . . with commendable sensitivity they had laid their fingers on the pulse of the age and prophesied according to that pulse. But I would have been—I must emphasize—endlessly grateful . . . if they themselves had been somewhat shocked over their findings and opposed to them a little moral criticism."[6]

A prophetic figure more complicated and richer in dialectical possibility—in psychologic and cultural implication—

is the Hieronymus, based on the figure of Savonarola, who appears in the story "Gladius Dei" and then later in the drama *Fiorenza*. Whereas Daniel walks in the rear guard of the backward devils, Hieronymus strides forward to meet us on the matters of "art" and "life," those perennial oppositions of Mann's concern. Hieronymus is also a charismatic political leader who incites the people of Florence against Medici rule. As we have come to expect, Mann takes no uncomplicated stance. Hieronymus is a fully ambivalent figure, unattractive in his fanaticism, impressive in his moral intractability; admirable in his hatred of privilege, hateful in his *ressentiment* and love of violence. He believes himself a scourge of God sent to punish the moral laxness of a misguided time; he is, in fact, an artist *manqué* turned demagogue whose will to power originates in frustrated sexuality and blocked creative urges. Accordingly, he preaches against art not as a crude and puritanical iconoclast but as a jealous artist denouncing the work of a despised rival.

Both "Gladius Dei" and the play *Fiorenza* conclude with stunning intimations of apocalypse. In "Gladius Dei" Hieronymus conjures up, against the thunder and lightning of a summer storm, a vision of God's sword visiting destruction on the "easy-going morality" and frivolous worship of art which reigned in Munich at the turn of the century. The end of *Fiorenza* shows Hieronymus moving forward to meet his historic destiny, unwilling to yield his power over Florence or to relax his will. Insanely in love with fate, he goes to the fire. Many years later (1938) Mann, in a brief essay called "Bruder Hitler," diagnosed Hitler in much the same way as he "psyched out" his Savonarola figure. Hitler was also an artist *manqué*, an incompetent painter and good-for-nothing Bohemian who enlarged his failures into a new myth of domination and absolute politics. We make no claim that Hieronymus "predicts" Hitler; only that Mann's concerns, in the decade preceding the First World War, were already directed toward those cultural aberrations which erupted into "the revolutionary-reactionary world" of totalitarian politics. Mann's interest in the Savonarola figure is compounded, as we noted, of fascination and repugnance; Hieronymus is an artist but also a demagogue, an ascetic but also the victim of fiercely repressed erotic impulses.

In "Bruder Hitler" Mann sets aside personal revulsion to examine Hitler in the light of his previous literary and cultural premonitions. Hitler appears a cruel distortion of those heroes—Tonio Kröger, Gustav von Aschenbach, Hieronymus—who agonized between art and life; who through the procedures of Mann's relentless psychologism showed themselves linked to the power of regressive myth. All this is ironic and deadly serious. He calls Hitler "A brother—a rather unpleasant and mortifying brother. He makes me nervous, the relationship is painful to a degree."[7] Mann "understands" Hitler as an artist of the irrational, a black magician whose powers derive from his ability to unleash the latent barbarism which is the dynamic underside of culture. And the derangement of character, the destiny which drew Hitler first toward European conquest and ultimately toward the immolation of Germany was the same that drew Hieronymus to the fire: the impulse toward domination and destruction which issues from intolerable self-hate. W. S. Merwin says this with extraordinary concentration in a one-line poem, an epitaph specifically for Hieronymus, generally for the alienated of every extremity:

SAVONAROLA
Unable to endure my world and calling the
failure God, I will destroy yours.

2

In *Civilization and Its Discontents* Freud clarifies the almost unbearable relationship existing between modern man and the culture in which he precariously survives. Freud approaches man and culture with his characteristic rational bias; his hope is to dredge up the unconscious so that fuller light may be shed over man's life in civilization—that this life may be made easier, more tolerable. Freud's interest in the dark side of the mind is a physician's concern: as Kenneth Burke puts it, ". . . a matter of human rescue." Although man lives in both light and darkness, his happiness lies under unclouded heaven. Lines from Schiller's *Der Taucher* (*The Diver*) come to Freud's mind:

> *He is happy*
> *Who breathes above in rose-colored light!*
> *But in the depths it is frightful,*
> *And man should not so tempt the gods*
> *And never, never crave to see*
> *What they graciously hide with horror and night.*

Yet mankind will, as Freud points out, tempt the gods who mercifully cover the depths. Man cannot resist peering into the abyss; he lives on the edge of chaos. Between man and the abyss is his defense against his own inner nature: his civilization and the complex social order within it. But he maintains civilization at great psychic cost. It demands repression and bitter renunciation. Men sacrifice their sexual life to worldly ambition; they drive toward business or professional success, withdrawing their love from wife and family. They suppress their innate savagery and attempt to live in peace with their neighbors. But the peace of the world is constantly threatened; Freud remarks, "In consequence of this primary mutual hostility of human beings, civilized society is perpetually threatened with disintegration."[8] As men renounce greater and greater parts of their instinctual nature for the sake of culture, they become anxious, conscience-stricken, hagridden with guilt. They suffer for the crimes which they have committed; they regret the crimes which remain uncommitted. Inhibitory mechanisms develop which inflame the original hostile tendencies: ". . . we may assert truly that in the beginning conscience arises through the suppression of an aggressive impulse, and that it is subsequently reinforced by fresh suppressions of the same kind."[9]

Freud sketches a gloomy picture. Man is a prisoner of his culture and a victim of his own nature. Culture exacts a high price in neurotic strain and feelings of personal guilt; man's instincts threaten to break through cultural barriers and engulf him in chaos. The ways of culture are sterile, constricting, finally unbearable; but immersion in instinctual chaos would mean the end of decent human conduct and eventually the end of life itself. It is a dilemma rich in tragic possibility, Aeschylean in conception. We see Clytemnestra, the irresistible force of instinct, meeting head-on Agamemnon, the immovable object of civilization. We know that civilization will endure, but not until the third play of the *Oresteia* do the gods decree for community, social order, and law. The Erinyes are not banished; they are metamorphosed into the Eumenides. The chthonic powers are not destroyed; through strenuous and unending effort they are brought under control and made useful. At any time they may break captivity and pursue mankind from Argos to Delphi, from Delphi to the ends of the earth.

Freud sees no easy or immediate solution to the problem he so uncompromisingly poses. He insists he is no enemy of culture, and discards as mere infantility the primitivisms which present themselves as remedies for an overcivilized world. Contrary to popular superstition, Freud gives no approval to uninhibited sexuality or "therapeutic" violence. He allows a single hope; in his fateful peroration to *Civilization and Its Discontents,* he ventures that "eternal Eros" may counteract the powers of darkness:

> The fateful question for the human species seems to me to be whether and to what extent their cultural development will succeed in mastering the disturbance of their communal life by the human instinct of aggression and self-destruction. It may be that in this respect precisely the present time deserves a special interest. Men have gained control over the forces of nature to such an extent that with their help they would have no difficulty in exterminating one another to the last man. They know this, and hence comes a large part of their current unrest, their unhappiness and their mood of anxiety. And now it is to be expected that the other of the two "Heavenly Powers," eternal Eros, will make an effort to assert himself in the struggle with his equally immortal adversary. But who can foresee with what success and with what result?[10]

Eternal Eros is libidinal force in the service of culture: the Erinyes turned Eumenides; or, as W. H. Auden puts it, "Eros, builder of cities." Eros is the energy which humanizes culture; it is the life-force seen working in nature, subverting the domain of aggression and death.

These speculations on culture are, of course, relevant to all the works in this study but particularly applicable to *Death in Venice* because that work faces, as uncompromisingly as Freud, impossible alternatives. Man can choose to live in his repressive culture and wither in impotence and neurotic despair; or he can succumb to instinct and be destroyed. Man, in brief, cannot live at peace in his culture; he dies without it. Mann explores the problem at greater length and with pointed historical explicitness in *The Magic Mountain* and *Doctor Faustus;* nowhere, however, does Mann achieve such a concentrated effect as he does in *Death in Venice.*

The story tells how an artist of great achievements and exemplary moral control breaks down under the strain of living beyond his psychic income. Gustav von Aschenbach represents the highest form of human being his culture can produce; he is, in a way, *Kultur* itself. He is a writer of refined intellectuality, a meticulous craftsman in prose. Aschenbach's approach to art, and also to life, is suggested by key words in the first paragraph. His creative work requires the utmost in *Behutsamkeit, Umsicht, Eindringlichkeit,* and *Genauigkeit.* Caution, tact, penetration, precision: these are the qualities of will which sustain Aschenbach. His art combines discipline and beauty; its very center is ethical control.

At the age of fifty and at the height of his fame, Aschenbach receives a mysterious summons to travel. He journeys to Venice where he is drawn to the sea and the beautiful young boy, Tadzio. The disciplined artist, the man whose life is seen in the image of the clenched fist and whose heroes are martyrs of self-control—St. Sebastian, Frederick the Great—falls catastrophically in love. He keeps his distance from Tadzio; the only contacts between them are glances and smiles, but the effect on Aschenbach is utterly destructive. His infatuation keeps him in the city during a plague of cholera; disease and love mingle and ripen together. Aschenbach dies in a vision; as he sinks down in death, the boy-god Tadzio laughingly beckons toward the sea.

Mann's narrative is enriched by thematic symbolisms, a powerful but always discreet allegorical implication, and hints of supernatural influence. The snub-nosed stranger who confronts Aschenbach in the Munich cemetery appears again in Venice as an unlicensed gondolier, and reappears toward the end of the story as a leering street-singer. He is death's messenger who kindles Aschenbach's *Wanderlust* and sends him to the plague-infected city; he is death's boatman who ferries him across the waters of Hades; finally he is the repellent musician reeking of carbolic acid—the stink of death—who sarcastically informs Aschenbach that there is indeed a plague in Venice.

Throughout the story Mann invokes Greek mythology and the Platonic philosophy of love and beauty. Mann does this not in the usual spirit of romantic Germanic Hellenism but in deliberate mockery of it. Aschenbach's love for Tadzio recalls the tender and ironic relationship between Socrates and Phaedrus; under the intellect-deadening power of the blazing sun and the reflecting sea, Aschenbach summons a picture of Athenian grace and beauty:

> . . . there was the ancient plane-tree outside the walls of Athens, a hallowed, shady spot, fragrant with willow-blossom and adorned with images and votive offerings in honour of the nymphs and Achelous. Clear ran the smooth-pebbled stream at the foot of the spreading tree. Crickets were fiddling. But on the gentle grassy slope, where one could lie yet hold the head erect, and shelter from the scorching heat, two men reclined, an elder with a younger, ugliness paired with beauty and wisdom with grace. Here Socrates held forth to youthful Phaedrus upon the nature of virtue and desire. . . .[11]

Later, when Aschenbach is demoniacally possessed by homosexual love and close to death, the words of the *Phaedrus* form involuntarily in his mind. It is Socrates' valediction to Phaedrus; when the older man warns the younger that the way of art is the way of emotional excess. It leads to the bottomless pit. Poets are wicked and dangerous fellows, not fit to instruct the young. The words echo in the mind of the sick and suffering Aschenbach as a fantastic irony, a mockery of his own pitiable condition. Socrates warns that even the highest devotion to beauty, the sternest self-discipline, and the strictest detachment—all the virtues distinguishing the civilized Aschenbach—lead to the abyss.

Mann tells us that the springs of artistic creation run underground in primitive energy and pre-conscious terror. Aschenbach dreams an obscene, Dionysian dream which stands in stark contrast to the Apollonian vision of Socrates and Phaedrus. He first witnesses, then participates in, a sexual orgy. Joining a savage group of revelers who circle around a monstrous phallus—the symbol of *Der fremde Gott,* the Stranger God—Aschenbach gets a shattering glimpse "of the wild beast nature that peers out in dreams." He descends into the chaos of the Id, into the world of unrestrained lust. And this vision comes to Aschenbach because he has so rigorously suppressed his own tendencies to disorder; because he has "renounced in a style of ideal purity Bohemianism and its muddy depths—renounced all sympathy with the abyss, and rejected the outcast and the depraved."

Aschenbach's degradation is bitterly ironic; he has become what he most deplores. But in his moral dissolution Aschenbach is vouchsafed tragic knowledge. He dies knowing that he has suffered punishment for denying his own nature. Aschenbach had always lived by, and even beyond, the ideals of his culture; his life was formed in the discipline of will and shaped by a rigid ethical credo: ". . . his motto was 'Hold fast' —he saw in his novel on Frederick the Great nothing less than the apotheosis of this command, which seemed to him the essence of passionate, suffering, and enduring virtue." Aschenbach's motto and his example, their embodiment in his self-sacrificing heroes—these were caught by the sympathetic imagination of his generation. His work seemed a citadel against anarchy; it showed an example that much could be saved—by effort of will alone—of an exhausted civilization living dangerously close to ruin.

Mann points out that Aschenbach's success as a writer derived from his ability to sense the spiritual direction of his times and to respond to the pressures of historical change. "In order that a creative work immediately exert some deep and general effect, there must exist a secret relationship, yes, a correspondence between the personal destiny of the author and the commonly shared destiny of his contemporaries."[12] Aschenbach had communicated with the underground sources of prophetic knowledge; his personal, psychologic destiny was soon to become public, political destiny.[13] The hero of the ethical will crumbles under the onslaughts of instinct and its demons; two years after *Death in Venice* appeared, the demons were loose all over Europe. A generation had expended its capital of psychic energy and could no longer endure the strain of sustained self-control. In 1914 civilization entered a period of prolonged crisis—a period in which the cultural super-ego has had little success in curbing instinctual aggression and those new and monstrous techniques for its expression.

3

For the world, I count it not an inn but an hospital; and a place not to live, but to die in.
                                 Sir Thomas Browne, *Religio Medici*

To shift from Freud's language to the terms of our particular preoccupation, we can say that historical fatality—embodied in world war, world revolution, and to bring it up to date, world-wide generational conflict—has loomed during the first half of our century as the determining element of existence. The writers of our study believed that not only should they possess that precious commodity of modernism, "a sense of their own age," but that they somehow could divine the nature of the concealed energies beneath the surface of events. Mann's *The Magic Mountain* offers a plenitude of knowledge and forgiveness, of prophetic hindsight and historical understanding; it is one of those monumental, synthetic works which both stuns and bores, impresses and exasperates. It is ineluctably *there,* an imaginary mountain with real problems and real people on it.

That a mountain is *there* has never seemed to me a compelling reason for scaling it. We require other fascinations: perhaps an evening's entertainment with Clavdia Chauchat, dinner at Mynheer Peeperkorn's groaning board, an encounter with those swordsmen (I should say gunmen) of dialectic, Settembrini and Naphta. We tend to obscure the full literary attractiveness of *The Magic Mountain* if we read it as a treatise. Mann rarely refuses the opportunities he offers himself to digress and expand, but we can refuse to be intimidated; we can skip and make those cuts Mann should have made. Perhaps our impatience with plenitude is only a matter of fashion; we now expect works of art to be concise, without that overfullness of explanation and example which Mann felt to be essential. And despite its length and enormous profusion of detail, *The Magic Mountain* is as closely structured as a Brahms symphony or a Wagner music drama. (Contrary to all partisan propaganda these nineteenth-century musicians are more alike than different and neither is the heir of Beethoven.) Like Brahms and Wagner, Mann is essentially a romantic lyricist turned symphonist; his prose "epics" progress through an accretion of minutely observed detail, through acute psychological penetration, through self-conscious employment of learned and difficult strategies.

All this complexity of procedure is qualified by Mann's celebrated and well-examined irony. (The best book on Mann—by Erich Heller—is called *Thomas Mann, the Ironic German*.) Mann's sophisticated use of irony recalls an anecdote told about Hans Reichenbach, the positivist and philosopher of scientific verification. He was leading a seminar which was exhaustively discussing probability as an ultimate yardstick to be laid against all human experience and all natural process. An exasperated student asked, "Professor Reichenbach, are you saying then that we live in a probable universe; that probability now replaces all traditional principles of order?" Reichenbach smiled and answered, "Probability is also only probable."

Mann's irony is also "only" ironic. I do not mean to underestimate Mann's two-edged approach to character and ideas: his fond belittling and fond admiration of Hans Castorp; his deliberate confounding of reaction and progress, of the positions of Naphta and Settembrini. Mann's attitude toward his own irony is that of the philosopher who warns us to be even skeptical of skepticism. Though he comes close through pervasive irony—which is not merely a matter of tone but a matter of total outlook—to annihilating the validity of his speculations and the possibilities of action, he does take positions that finally mediate between dialectical extremes. These are "counterpositions," temporary resting places from which to proceed toward further mediations. The questing spirit must move on, toward that Absolute which Hegel saw as man's goal in the historical world. Irony is neither for Mann an escape from commitment nor does it—as unfriendly critics have alleged—issue from a perverse refusal to make up his mind. Mann believes that the artist must transcend all partisan emotion, "all irritable striving after fact," and stick to his job of "objective contemplation—in a word, [of] the irony which I have long since recognized as the native element of all creative art."[14] Eliot surely had similar thoughts in mind when he remarked, to much critical dismay, that a writer could treat his ideals in prose but that in poetry he could only deal with the actual.

We might treat the actuality of *The Magic Mountain* through some observations Nietzsche once made on Wagner's overture to the *Meistersinger:*

> I heard once again—as if for the first time—Richard Wagner's overture to the *Meistersinger.* That is a gorgeous, overladen, heavy, and late art which has the pride to suppose that two centuries of music are comprehensible and still alive. It does honor to the Germans that such pride did not miscalculate. What humours and powers, what seasons and climates are not mixed here! . . . It flows broad and full: and suddenly there is an instant of obscure hesitation, as if a chasm opened up between cause and effect, a pressure which makes us dream, almost a nightmare . . . even a certain coarseness that is underlined, as if the artist wished to tell us: "that is part of my intention"; a ponderous drapery, something despotic and barbaric and solemn; a flurry of learned and respectable riches and lace; something German in the best and worst sense of the word: German in its variousness, formlessness, plenitude; a certain German strength and richness of soul which has no fear of concealing itself behind the refine-

ments of decadence—which perhaps feels best there; a genuine augury of the German soul which is both young and out of date, both overripe and overrich in its future. This kind of music expresses best how I regard the Germans: they belong to the day before yesterday and the day after tomorrow—*as yet they have no today.*[15]

To approach *The Magic Mountain* through Nietzsche and Wagner is more than a convenient critical stratagem; it gets to the heart of Mann's concerns about culture and nihilism, the impossible alternatives of the historical situation. Like Nietzsche, Mann maintained a love-hate affair with Wagner all his life. He parodied Wagner in the two early stories, "Tristan," and "Blood of the Walsungs"; he apotheosized him in two substantial essays; and during his years of exile, he declared that Wagner's work was "created and directed against 'civilization,' against the entire culture and society dominant since the Renaissance. . . ."[16] Nietzsche's mixture of admiration and insight apply with uncanny precision to *The Magic Mountain*. The novel, "gorgeous, overladen, heavy," carries an immense weight of the European past: of historical understanding and revaluation; it recapitulates a century of European spiritual history and brings it to novelistic life. Throughout the novel Mann pauses to instruct us in what he is doing—as if the reader might suffer from that same charming obtuseness which afflicts Hans Castorp. At certain *stretti* in the novel—"Walpurgis Night," "Snow," "Highly Questionable"—Mann opens the chasm separating humanity from the country of the undersoul and from Hell itself. And *The Magic Mountain* is German, *echt deutsch,* "in the best and worst sense of the word."

Here we must proceed with caution. Mann's work has been codified and systematized in criticism and scholarship; it stands before us, as does the work of the other modern masters, as something akin to scripture, complete and apparently seamless. We are tempted to read *The Magic Mountain* as a prelude to *Doctor Faustus* and to take both books as a single parable of German historical destiny. The apocalyptic fate of Adrian Leverkühn then appears as a sequel to Hans Castorp's story. But *The Magic Mountain* belongs "to the day before yesterday," to that first moment of modernism when the intellectual and artistic world of Europe was receiving the shock waves of the new irrationalisms in philosophy and psychology, the new disorders in painting, music, and literature.

Mann started work on *The Magic Mountain* in the fall of 1913. It was begun in the midst of revolutionary developments in artistic style, a "qualitative break" with old forms and procedures. Arnold Schönberg published his first atonal compositions in 1910; Diaghilev produced Igor Stravinsky's *Petrouchka* in 1910, his *Le Sacre du Printemps* in 1913. The Cubist movement in painting reached its apogee at the Armory Show of 1913. Ezra Pound and his friends issued the marching orders for modern poetry in their *Imagist Manifesto* of 1913. In Italy Emilio Marinetti was busy explaining and marketing Futurism; in Germany the "glorification of the 'modern' for its own sake and the vague desire for some kind of extreme innovation preceded the positive achievements of the new generation."[17] The war put all this burgeoning life into a period of suspended animation, but the decade of the twenties saw its spectacular revival. Mann completed *The Magic Mountain* in September 1924 and it was published in November of the same year. It has taken its place among the other works we recognize as classics of modernism and which appeared at the same time: Eliot's *The Waste Land*, Hemingway's first and greatest novel, *The Sun Also Rises*, Joyce's *Ulysses*, Rilke's *Duineser Elegien* and *Die Sonette an Orpheus*.

The relationship of *The Magic Mountain* to modernism, like everything else about Mann's work and life, is not easy to define. Mann tells the story of Hans Castorp in a way perfectly consonant with nineteenth-century novelistic techniques. He does not scramble temporal sequences; he is a traditional "omniscient author," manipulating his characters from on high; he interrupts his narrative with asides about his characters and their predicaments; he frequently "tells" rather than "shows." And so on. But Mann's traditional technique is an elaborate disguise. His heritage, his modernist qualifications descend straight from a prime source. His musical repetitions, his use of the leitmotiv; his brilliant handling of recurrent symbolism; his pervasive underscoring of the actual with the mythical—all most aggressively "modern"—flow from Wagner whom Nietzsche named the very essence of modernity.[18]

Equally modern is Mann's treatment of the generic conventions of pastoral. *The Magic Mountain* is set in a sanatorium remote from the "flatland," in an atmosphere close to death but also rich in therapeutic possibilities. Time is distorted, rendered "mythic" and deprived of the sense of measured sequence which distinguishes historical time. The world of the Berghof is a community of the suffering and the dying; its style of life parodies a simple existence close to nature, to the gods, and to spiritual truth. The patients eat and gossip, make love and endlessly attend to themselves. They propitiate a host of lesser deities through what seem trivial or malign rites. They play at psychoanalysis and spiritualism; they are possessed with devils and run wild with hysteria. They try endlessly to amuse themselves and when amusements fail they lapse into boredom or snarling dementia. A higher god, Mynheer Peeperkorn, appears among them and dispenses a strangely inarticulate gospel of vitalism. Through all this, Hans Castorp pursues his education with bourgeois diligence and Germanic thoroughness. He approaches knowledge and experience with wide-eyed amazement; his observations often have the shrewdness which characterizes the astringent remarks of the rustics who appear in Shakespeare's pastoral comedies.

The Magic Mountain is tainted pastoral set in that remote age before our Iron Times. Historical process is suspended while Hans Castorp pauses for seven years to "meet us honestly" on culture and politics, and on what goes deeper than either, the mythic underside of existence. The Berghof, like Gerontion's boarding house, is polyglot and international; its patients are Europeans and Orientals, Gentiles and Jews, humanists from Italy and charming Karamazovs from east of the Caucasus. All are ill; all are afflicted with the fever and hysteria of their disease. Many, like Hans and his cousin Joachim, are in their early twenties or younger; tuberculosis is a disease of youth. Disease heightens the intensity of discussion and closes the gap between rationality—the mind operating with cultural awareness and ethical control—and the unconscious—the mind operating under the stimulation of instinct. The Berghof has the freedom of a community released from the usual repressions of social life.

The omnipresence of death makes trivial the ordinary concerns of vocation and ambition. We are occasionally reminded of Hans's profession by Settembrini's sardonic "Herr Engineer"; but this reminder always pulls us up short. Hans never opens his big book on marine architecture and nothing in his mental preoccupations indicates interest in his profession or in the pursuit of a career. Hans's vocation is the assiduous cultivation of his sickness, his rich and full life as a patient. He has, as Hofrat Behrens tells him, a talent for illness; and once aware of his *petite tache humide,* he devotes himself to the complicated, time-killing, and narcissistic regimen of his "cure." Disease isolates him not only for self-indulgent cultivation of inwardness, but for bringing him closer to the mysterious processes of life:

> Interest in death and disease, in the pathological, in decay, is only one form of expression for interest in life, in the human being, as the humanistic faculty of medicine shows. He who is interested in organic life is particularly interested in death; it might be a good subject for a novel concerned with the education of the human being to show that the experience of death is in the last analysis an experience of life; that it leads to the human.[19]

Mann said this in an overtly political speech defending the new and very unstable Weimar Republic. Hans's education on *The Magic Mountain* leads from death to a vision of life and back to death again. History interrupts his education but in the midst of action, on a battlefield of the First World War, he is sustained by what he has learned.

Human corruption began in knowledge, but without knowledge we are cut off from the possibilities of redemption. Hans acquires the knowledge which can earn forgiveness. His education begins with the recognition of his illness, that is, with the discovery of self on the physical and natural level. After the excitement of realizing he owns a body with an intricate physiology and chemistry, he then discovers sexuality and love. Clavdia Chauchat initiates Hans into the erotic mysteries; Mann generates a mounting tension of sexual excitement which is finally released in the section called "Walpurgis Night." The juxtaposition of serious reflection on the meaning of history and culture with erotic preoccupation recalls *Gerontion* and *The Waste Land*. Making love and understanding history are interdependent activities. We remember in *Gerontion*

> *Fräulein von Kulp*
> *Who turned in the hall, one hand on the door.*

At the conclusion of "Walpurgis Night," the love-stricken Hans watches Clavdia:

> ". . . she slipped from her chair, and glided over the carpet to the door, where she paused an instant, framed in the doorway; half turned toward him, with one bare arm lifted high, her hand upon the hinge. Over her shoulder she said softly: '*N'oubliez pas de me rendre mon crayon.*' And went out."[20]

Unlike Gerontion, Hans follows Clavdia through the door, ". . . made [her] acquaintance and then returned so much later to his chamber than the duty-loving Joachim to his."[21]

Hans's two ideological preceptors, Naphta and Settembrini, maintain a degraded relationship with sexuality. Naphta, like Hieronymus whom he resembles, lives as an ascetic, but affords himself a luxuriously appointed apartment and expensive clothes. His asceticism derives from harshly repressed sexual urges, and the ferocity of his opinions is that of a hysteric. Settembrini, in a parody of Latin lecherousness, ogles the girls in a way that shocks the properly brought-up Hans. Settembrini's relation to the erotic is healthier than Naphta's; it is, however, more superficial, less charged with that sense of guilt and mystery which makes Hans's love of Clavdia a perilous but always intriguing spiritual adventure.

The ideological struggles between Naphta and Settembrini push the politics of reaction and liberalism to logical absurdity—and further, to ultimate violence. They are not, however, simply stylized representatives of their respective points of view. Their political attitudes are the expression of personal disorder and deep psychic distress; they are sick men, and their sickness affects both the substance and form of their discourse. Settembrini's fervor carries him to the *reductio* of liberal hope in redemptive politics. He believes in a United Europe brought together through the fellowship of learning and literature. He is also a fire-breathing Italian patriot; he cannot forget his country's quarrel with Austria and the problem of the Tyrol. Much of the shallowness of liberalism is revealed in Settembrini's advocacy: its easy optimism about progress; its refusal to acknowledge the existence of evil; its hope that reason will prevail in human affairs. But his saving grace—which is both a quality of his mind and his style in action—is that he is never less than human.

Naphta is a more complex figure. By origin a Galician Jew, by training a Jesuit, and by conviction a Marxist revolutionary, he seems the embodiment of irreconcilables, a provoking spirit of contradiction. He believes in absolute evil and hence in absolute repression. For him politics is not the sustaining of an ethical human community, education not "the daughter of enlightenment." Education is unrelieved discipline, the violent repression of personality, absolute obedience; politics, in its ideal form, must become Terror:

> "No," Naphta went on. "Liberation and development of the individual are not the key to our age, they are not what our age demands. What it needs, what it wrestles after, what it will create—is Terror."
>
> He uttered the last word lower than the rest; without a motion of his body. Only his eye-glasses suddenly flashed. All three of them [Hans, Joachim, Settembrini], as they heard it, jumped . . .[22]

Naphta is not always so blunt in his speech, nor is Mann's prophecy and critique of approaching totalitarianism always so explicit. Naphta has the craftiness and formidable intellectual prowess popularly attributed to the Jesuits. Settembrini warns Hans to be on his guard; he knows that Naphta is more than a prize-winning debater: he is a positive danger.

Naphta owns two absolutes, his rhetorical power and his will. His arguments triumph over Settembrini's humanism; Naphta's bitter logic pushes each of Settembrini's positions around to its opposite. Naphta "demonstrates" that true freedom is total obedience; that true progress is reaction; that even the Revolution made in the name of Liberty, Fraternity, and Equality had only equivocal ramifications. In the end Naphta demonstrates that his logical method is an empty form, a container for the spiritual void. His very last ideological protestation is this harrowing revelation: "Only out of radical skepsis, out of moral chaos, does the Absolute arise, the holy Terror which the age demands." *Our nada who art in nada, nada be thy name.* . . . We see Mann's purpose in giving Naphta Jewish origins, Jesuitical education, aesthetic predilections, revolutionary fanaticism. Each valid element in the ideological medley is canceled by an equally valid element. The result is nihilism.

Will and nihilism make the familiar politics of totalitarianism. As has been often noted, totalitarian politics has no substance but the Terror prophesied by Naphta; no purpose other than to maintain itself in power. Like Naphta's steel-edged dialectic which perverts everything into its opposite, totalitarianism distorts democratic and socialist ideals until they are devoid of humanistic content. Totalitarianism must incite and promulgate Terror until Terror, observing the logic of its own devising, destroys itself. Naphta belongs among the backward devils. He is a false prophet not because his being and thought do not typify what came to pass; Naphta has "clear knowledge of his organic function" and interprets correctly the Chaldean script before him. But like Spengler, who urged men to join with the powers of darkness, Naphta passionately allies himself to an evil destiny. Mann makes it clear that prophecy is a high moral calling, that it must take critical form, and that it must not conspire to bring about the catastrophe it warns against.

When the First World War breaks into the isolated world of the Berghof, Hans responds with incredulity. The war was "that historic thunder-peal, of which we speak with bated breath, [which] made the foundations of the earth to shake; but for us it was the shock that fired the mine beneath the magic mountain, and set our sleeper ungently outside the gates. Dazed he sits in the long grass and rubs his eyes—a man who, despite many warnings, had neglected to read the papers."[23] History comes to Hans as a shocking and incredible intrusion. He had long ago adjusted to a mode of life divested of the burdens of time; he had neglected to have his smashed pocket-watch repaired and had given up consulting calendars. Without clock and calendar and newspapers, he achieved his hermetic freedom to live in "the on-going Eternal Always."

Hans is surprised at the terrible gift of History, but his education on the Magic Mountain has been devoted to the acquisition of that knowledge, terrible though it may be, which points to the acceptance of and liberation from history. The strife of the counterpositions, the elaborate dialectic of life and death—which is no simple dualism but tragic actuality—achieves mediation in Hans's "dream poem of humanity." He does not dream his dream as a private person; he is a recording instrument receiving a message from *Anima Mundi:*

> Now I know that it is not out of our single souls we dream. We dream anonymously and communally, if each after his fashion. The great soul of which we are a part may dream through us, in our manner of dreaming, its own secret dreams, of its youth, its hope, its joy and peace— and its blood-sacrifice.[24]

We recall Hans's communal dream. He walks in an Arcadian landscape among a race of gravely dignified young men and women. In this untainted pastoral setting there flowers a society based on mutual respect and affection. But co-existing with order, beauty, and love in this golden world is its regressive underside. Hans witnesses the blood sacrifice: two half-naked hags dismember and devour a young child. On the level of literal symbolism, this is a chillingly apt image for the First World War and its slaughter of an entire generation of European youth. Hans interprets his dream more broadly. (Or, we must say, Mann interprets it for him.

Hans allows his dream to slip from the surface of his conscious mind.) In the illuminated state to which he awakes, however, he can see all life, all existence in stunning clarity.

It is human goodness and love which mediate between the counterpositions. Hans rejects Naphta's "*guazzabuglio* of God and the Devil" as the religion of death devoted to the absolute dominion of the blood sacrifice. He rejects Settembrini's religion of reason as the stunted child of humanism; reason by itself is inadequate to deal with The Terror. Settembrini's blasts on "his small horn of reason" will not exorcize the devils from madmen. Reason too easily reverts to its opposite; political and social revolutions made in the name of reason have notoriously concluded with Naphta's rule of Terror. Hans proposes a radical humanism in which love and goodness, never forgetting the unholy existence of the blood sacrifice, transcend both the Apollonian control of reason and the Dionysian frenzy of aggression. Or to return to Freud's language, Hans has a vision of Eternal Eros asserting himself against his immortal adversary.

4

An end is come, the end is come: it
watcheth for thee; behold, it is come.
Ezekiel 7:6. Text for Adrian
Leverkühn's *Apocalypsis cum figuris.*

If *The Magic Mountain* is pastoral, *Doctor Faustus* is apocalypse, "a myth of the end of the world." If *The Magic Mountain* reveals a vision of love mediating between reason and terror, *Doctor Faustus* shows a great artist and the world he represents succumbing to radical evil. Mann's method, always complex, treats the story of Adrian Leverkühn on many levels; or, speaking musically, in many voices, rhythmic and melodic transformations, and instrumental textures. *Faustus* is biography and autobiography, personal confession, a textbook of musical theory, political and cultural allegory, apocalyptic myth, and high prophetic anguish. Three tercets from the *Inferno* (Canto II) stand on the title-page; we are reminded that we not only begin a journey through Hell but undertake a work which is, in Dante's sense, richly *polysemous.*

We shall keep in mind, then, Dante's scheme of four-fold interpretation: namely, that a text may be read on literal, allegoric, moral, and anagogic levels. The literal level concerns itself with what we read on the title-page, *The Life of the German Composer Adrian Leverkühn Told by a Friend*. The allegoric level concerns itself primarily with the intricate metaphoric implications of music: with Adrian's compositions as a complex symbol for modern cultural reality. The moral is hardly a "level" of *Faustus;* at myriad places Mann strikes through his narrator's mask, loses his cool, and calls down God's thunderbolts on the seducers and traducers of his country. Similarly, anagogy as the concern with typology and "last things," and with the relationship of past and present, permeates the book.

I mention Dante's scheme of interpretation but do not use it for lopping or stretching. Mann himself uses it to interpret his story as he tells it. No work of Mann is so agonizingly self-conscious; he writes the critique of Faustus simultaneously with the text.[25] Dante's scheme also brings into prominence the medieval *cantus firmus* moving beneath the book's modern polyphony. Adrian is not Goethe's wide-eyed striver but Marlowe's persistent sinner, the Faust of the Lutheran Reformation. Mann sees the Reformation in the terms of his revolutionary-reactionary paradigm; Serenus Zeitblom notes, "I like to compare the Reformation to a bridge which not only links our world of free thought with the age of scholasticism but also and equally leads back into the middle ages." Although the figure of Faust has come to symbolize modern or post-Renaissance man, he is essentially a transitional figure: a man with "advanced" views whose thought and actions prophesy a world yet to come.

Adrian Leverkühn enters the musical world of the late nineteenth century and devises a radical restructuring of musical technique. He "breaks through" tonal and harmonic expressiveness to new contrapuntal discipline; he overturns the conventional affective symbolism of consonance and dissonance. His *Apocalypsis cum figuris*

> ". . . is dominated by the paradox (if it is a paradox) that in it dissonance stands for the expression of every-

thing lofty, solemn, pious, everything of the spirit; while consonance and firm tonality are reserved for the world of hell, in this context a world of banality and common-place."[26]

And in his "breakthrough," in his revolutionary achievement of craft, Adrian returns music to the past. His techniques—his retrograde canons, his weaving of symbolic letters into the musical fabric, his strict forms of variation, and his uses of modal scales and organum—all derive from an earlier period in music history.

Adrian's revolutionary-reactionary attack on nineteenth-century musical procedures is based on a particular interpretation of historical process. He argues with his friend and Boswell, Zeitblom, that the history of music has a prefigured teleology, an inner destiny. The nineteenth century exhausted the forms perfected in the eighteenth; sonata and fugue (in the tonal form developed by Bach) are no longer "possible." Also determined for Adrian is his predilection for music dependent on literary texts. He thus explains the intimate linking of his music with words: ". . . the entire development of German music strove toward the word-*cum*-tone drama of Wagner, and there discovered its goal." "One goal," counters Zeitblom and offers Brahms as an example of a nineteenth-century composer who managed to use the old forms and did not violate his instrumental music with literary programs—with words.

Mann pushes and pulls on the question of freedom and determinism. If Adrian is not free to compose except in his radical atonal style, then he is a victim of History. History has used up the art-forms of the previous age; History has brought a hegemony of the word into musical work. From Beethoven's Ninth Symphony to Mahler's *Das Lied von der Erde,* from Wagner to Schönberg's *Gurrelieder,* the word exerted its determining influence on music. From Wagner's *Tristan* to Schönberg's *Verklärte Nacht,* traditional harmony moved through a process of chromatic dissolution toward the eventual abandonment of tonality and key relationships. These developments were required by the nature of music itself, by the demands of structure and technique and not, as the devil reminds us, "by social conditions." Here Mann puts the questionable doctrine of aesthetic fatalism into the devil's mouth. The devil tells Adrian (Chapter XXV) that the tonal procedures of the nineteenth century are forbidden to modern composers because they have become clichés ". . . through a historical process which no one reverses." It is also the devil who outlines views which are, to the reader of Mann, very familiar indeed. He tells Adrian that the modern artist cannot approach the old generic forms except in a spirit of critique and parody. Echoing Nietzsche's prophecy that art in an age of excessive historical awareness becomes self-conscious and *critical,* the devil mockingly consoles Adrian: "Art becomes critique—something very much worthy of respect, who denies it?" Mann has, of course, practiced the art of stylistic and mythic parody; he has devoted many pages of his fictional work to exhaustive critique. Is Mann, then, of the devil's party and unaware of it?

We can firmly say that Mann is unaware of nothing. He understands the treacherous appeal to historical process and the supple confusions implicit in the doctrine that says because a thing happened it *had* to happen. Zeitblom is revolted by the Kridwiss circle because its acceptance of political barbarism was based on a slimy opportunism which, having calculated the direction of history, then proceeds to welcome it as "inevitable." Mann also points up the equivocal relationship between cultural barbarism and Adrian's revolutionary music. The devil describes Adrian's musical "breakthrough" in language heavily prophetic of Hitler's New Order:

> Know, then, we pledge you the success of that which with our help you will accomplish. You will lead the way, you will strike up the march of the future, the lads will swear by your name, who thanks to your madness will no longer need to be mad. On your madness they will feed in health, and in them you will become healthy. Do you understand? Not only will you break through the paralysing difficulties of the time—you will break through time itself, by which I mean the cultural epoch and its cult, and dare to be barbaric, twice barbaric indeed, because of coming after the humane, after all possible root-treatment and bourgeois raffinement.[27]

As the devil raves, he passes imperceptibly from prophesying the course of Adrian's musical development to urging a German political destiny. He no longer speaks of music but of a new era of myth, passion, and blood; a new "cult" which will repudiate middle-class refinements: humanity, liberalism, personal freedom and the other supposedly worn-out ideals of a decadent culture.

Mann makes it easy for us to understand Adrian's music as the devil's invention, a symbol of totalitarian ideology and its demands for the renunciation of freedom. Mann also suggests Adrian's music is *his* music, a symbol for everything his work stands for: its elaborate thematic structure, its relentlessly critical treatment of culture, its parodistic syle. Does Mann, in effect, indict himself in *Doctor Faustus?* Much critical confusion has resulted in attempts to answer this question. We can weakly say, "yes and no"; invoke the principle of the identity of opposites; talk about Mann's dialectical inscrutability. We come to no secure conclusion if we remain frozen on the allegoric level. But on the moral level Adrian's life and art—that ambiguously savage and utterly spiritual music—may be viewed as expiations for what Germany inflicted on the world. Evil of the Nazi kind cannot be forgotten, forgiven, or taken back: it can only be atoned for.

We hear Mann's agony on every page. How did Germany, *das Land der Dichter und Denker* become (in Karl Kraus's sardonic distortion) *das Land der Richter und Henker?* How could the land of Kant and Hegel, Schiller and Goethe, Bach and Beethoven spawn the regime of Hitler, Goebbels, and Streicher; promulgate the blood purges; maintain the ghastly death camps? Who or what was to blame for "the dictatorship of the scum"? In desperation Mann applies hindsight in a most perilous undertaking: the fixing of historical guilt. The determinism informing Adrian's discussion of music history also torments Mann's arraignment of the German past. He sees the Reformation and its resurgence of medieval demonism making a permanent contribution to the underside of German religious life. He sees Luther's positive acceptance of secular authority contributing to the German passion for obedience, and establishing German political destiny, its drive toward the extremities of revolution and reaction. Mann examines other aspects of German history. *Blut und Boden* emphasis on *das Volk* inflamed the German tendency toward political irrationalism. Nietzsche, who is everywhere present in *Doctor Faustus,* served the Nazis as an ideological hero. Wagner gave the Nazis a folk religion and a racial theory.

This historical evidence is "strictly" composed into the thematic texture of *Doctor Faustus.* On nearly any page we hear a familiar motif, or its expansion, diminution, or inversion. The cumulative effect leaves the reader protesting, as Zeitblom protests Adrian's twelve-tone method, that *Faustus* was already written before Mann wrote it; that he brought no freedom to the book but only followed the strict logic of his musical-dialectical method. And the implication is strong that there is no more freedom in history than in Adrian's music where every note falls into its necessary contrapuntal relationship, "and no note is free." Luther and the Reformation, the German character, romantic-mythic emphasis on the folk, the hammer blows of Nietzsche's critique of all values: all fitted into a predetermined historical context and made the Nazi state an inevitable historical phenomenon.

Thus it appeared to Mann during the years 1943–1946. All the stresses of overwhelming guilt, shame, and despair shaped the apocalyptic fiction of *Doctor Faustus. The Magic Mountain* ends on the battlefields of the First World War; but Mann could imagine some mediation of the historical crisis, a further (although unglimpsed) turning of the dialectical process which would set the world moving toward love and community. The sacrifice of blood would be the necessary tribute men pay—through the release of destructive action— for controlling the demonic. In *The Magic Mountain* Mann stands with the biblical prophets, proclaiming expiation through suffering, tempering words of doom with tidings of possible redemption. After the testing of souls, a new historical chapter can begin. But in *Doctor Faustus* Mann stands with the biblical apocalyptists, facing a radically different situation. It is too late for history to change its course; the apocalyptic message announces "Creation has grown old."[28] The end of time and history is imminent or has already come to pass. In such a predicament men no longer make historical choices. History is now fatality; historical process a deadly movement toward the end of movement. ". . . whenever man shudders before the menace of his own work and longs to flee from the radically demanding historical hour, there he finds himself near to the apocalyptic vision of a process that cannot be arrested."[29]

Mann enforces the apocalyptic thrust of *Doctor Faustus* with three distinct endings. We watch with Serenus Zeitblom as Nazi Germany stumbles into its final abyss of horror; we watch with Adrian as he collapses into paralytic madness—at the end of his allotted twenty-four years; we listen to the end of *Dr. Fausti Weheklag,* Adrian's last and greatest work, and its cello fermata on high G. Only in Adrian's music—the play within the play—does Mann suggest that the apocalypse might be transcended. This music divests itself of all parody and self-imposed "objectivity"; it returns to new (and old) expressiveness. Here we can say that Mann turns back from the apocalyptic to the prophetic. Here the hope beyond hope, "the miracle which goes beyond belief," offers itself: that turning away from History as irrational force breaking the necks of men, and toward history as the power reestablishing the world. For the true prophet receives those messages which assure men new beginnings are possible and new stages of existence attainable. He does not have foreknowledge of what the future holds, but he urges faith in "a significance for man's way in the world."[30] Of all Mann's works, indeed, of all modern novels, *Doctor Faustus* most deeply questions this significance. But the answer, like Adrian's final cello tone, remains as a light in the darkness.

Afterword

> "We overstep history when man becomes present to us in
> his most exalted works, through which he has been able . . .
> to catch Being in motion . . . What has here been done by
> men, who allowed themselves to be absorbed by the eternal
> truth which became language through them, although it
> wears an historical garb, is above and beyond history. . . ."
> —Karl Jaspers, *The Origin and Goal of History*

After the apocalypse—the theatre of the absurd, the existential
novel, the poetry of silence. *Doctor Faustus* is among the last
works of "classic modernism" to engage the tragic power of
history. During the fifties and through the middle years of the
sixties, writers backed away from the world of public action.
The issues were muddled; past friends became present enemies, past enemies became present friends. Political ideologies,
formerly differentiated into "fascistic" and "democratic," de-
generated into rhetorical confusion. Writers who once made
extravagant appeals to *History* reconsidered and some recanted.
The word itself proved a source of embarrassment. W. H.
Auden deleted "Spain" from his *Collected Shorter Poems*
largely because of its menacing last two lines: "History to the
defeated/May say Alas but cannot help or pardon." On this
formulation of Hegel's dictum that *Die Weltgeschichte ist das
Weltgericht* ("world history is the world court of justice"),
Auden comments, "To say this is to equate goodness with success. It would have been bad enough if I had ever held this
wicked doctrine, but that I should have stated it simply be-

cause it sounded to me rhetorically effective is quite inexcusable."[1]

When Auden wrote "Spain" (1937) he was acting out pro-Loyalist sympathies and expressing Marxist hope that events were moving toward an inevitable victory for the Revolution. (Marx himself put it most crudely in a letter to Engels: "History is the judge; its executioner, the proletarian."[2]) Other lines in "Spain" appeal to the violent and vengeful process generated by "History the operator, the/Organiser. Time the refreshing river." Such an appeal stimulated (and can still stimulate) a powerful response; it disturbed the underground pool of assumptions fed by the intellectual and emotional experience of a thoroughly historicized age. The "rhetorical effectiveness" of Auden's *History* depended on the susceptibility of Auden's readers in the thirties; the mere mention of the word evoked a terrified sense of participation in events of global significance—a quasi-religious experience.

Auden's appeal to *History* is a dramatic (and from Auden's present repentant stance) perhaps immoral instance of what Arthur Lovejoy calls "metaphysical pathos." Lovejoy speaks of ". . . the eternalistic pathos—the aesthetic pleasure which the bare abstract idea of immutability gives us."[3] He shows how Shelley's *Adonais* appealed to the belief that a world of unchanging forms was both delicious and desirable. We might say that Auden's appeal to *History* constitutes a *pathos of mutability;* as the bare abstract idea of immutability stimulated in Shelley's readers its particular and powerful response, so the idea of devastating change earns, in an age permeated by historicism, almost automatic intellectual assent. A metaphysical pathos depends on current intellectual fashions and prejudices; its use doubtless may be morally questionable. However, to come to Auden's defence against himself, his appeal to *History* does not necessarily show him the heartless purveyor of "wicked doctrine"; rather, it shows him as he has always been: a hero of the *Zeitgeist,* fully aware of changing conditions in the intellectual climate.

It is not easy to determine where the use of a concept for "rhetorical effectiveness"—as metaphysical pathos—ends and its use as controlling principle begins. A crucial concern of this study has been to explain the prevalent occasions of history as metaphysical pathos. When Eliot urges that

> *History has many cunning passages, contrived corridors*
> *And issues, deceives with whispering ambitions . . .*

he makes a specific appeal to our presuppositions about history as a determined, misleading, and mysterious agency. But Eliot's appeal is enlarged by other awarenesses and qualified by an incisive moral skepticism. Another concern carries this study beyond *History* as metaphysical pathos and toward an understanding of how history informs literary imagination in more comprehensive ways. Certain poems and novels display Nietzschean or Marxist apocalyptism; others express hope for some form of mediation—a reconciliation of opposing forces. For the dubious purpose of a tidy conclusion, our six writers might be placed under two headings: Nietzscheans and Hegelians. Hegelians see in history an unending dialectical struggle; they tally up the costs of action; they explore the limitations of culture. Believing history to be inseparable from existence, they speculate that "Only through time time is conquered"; that in the dialectical process the elements of negation may be overcome and the line of existence move toward a better human fate. The path of mediation splits off to right and left. *Four Quartets* recalls the theological implications of Hegel's mediations; its Christian accommodation moves to the right. *Man's Fate* moves toward the left and sees, despite grave contradictions, an improved social order following the agonies of revolutionary crisis.

Nietzscheans turn away from the path of mediation and seek "anti-historical" interpretations for the meaning of temporal existence. They devise mythical explanations for the clash of historical energies and tend to deny the importance of the social realm. Society and its institutional orders inhibit the individual self struggling toward some higher order of being—a personal transcendence of history. Nietzschean mythologies, although often developed with a penumbra of religious implication, make no supernatural claims; rather, they become metaphors expressing the deep psychological need to *overcome* history. The most radical overcoming of history is the denial of its existence; or, since the Nietzschean way is the way of contradiction, a proclamation that the history which does not exist will shortly come to its destined end.

However, we cannot say that our writers are purely Nietzscheans or Hegelians. Yeats is perhaps closest to Nietzsche, Eliot closest to Hegel. But Yeats absorbs some of his dialectical cunning from Hegelianism; Eliot shows a skepticism toward knowledge reminiscent of Nietzsche. At most, we can point out that certain works display qualities of mediation we think of as Hegelian; other works, operating against the stresses of the ongoing historical situation, display a Nietzschean disbelief in redemptive processes and a despairing (but sometimes hopeful) apocalyptism. *Doctor Faustus* is the most Nietzschean performance of modern literature; it is, to be sure, an extreme case which ". . . does not so much follow in [Nietzsche's] footsteps as over his body."[4] Malraux's work begins and ends with Nietzsche. The two early books push a hard-line Nietzscheanism and emphasize Will-to-Power, existential despair, and *übermenschliche* posturings. *The Walnut Trees of Altenburg* gives us Nietzsche the radical humanist who, having announced the death of God, now apotheosizes the immortal "quality of Man."

I have made no attempt to conceal my own position. While acknowledging the literary power, the profound symbolic resonance of the apocalyptic view, I have devoted more favorable attention to those works which, however tentatively, seek the way of mediation. The contrived corridor of history is man's inescapable destiny—but a destiny conceived (manufactured, if you will) by human consciousness limited by its own psychological frontiers. Historical destiny—whether Hegel's Absolute or Nietzsche's apocalypse—is not a "fact" of existence; it is an interpretation forced on individuals, groups, and whole cultures living in a period of unremitting historical change. Both systematic philosophies of history and literary fictions denoting historical process "interpret" the facts of human experience in history. To my way of feeling and thinking, certain interpretations make the greater claim on the moral imagination. The *Anima Mundi* revealed to Hans Castorp "a dream poem of humanity," to Yeats a Rough Beast. "The Second Coming" is the work of a great poet, *The Magic Mountain* the work of a great poet who extended his sympathies beyond the frontiers of art.

Perhaps such a distinction carries us outside the boundaries of "proper" literary criticism and its meticulous concern with the work itself. I have shamelessly diverted attention from the work itself to what the work *points at*.[5] Which does not mean I have read poems and novels for their pragmatic "relevance" or as simple-minded social commentary. I have tried to read these poems and novels as a record of spiritual preoccupation, to show how six writers understood (or tried to understand), overcame (or tried to overcome) history. Lines from Eliot's *Little Gidding* might serve as an assessment of their efforts:

> . . . *This is the use of memory:*
> *For liberation —not less of love but expanding*
> *Of love beyond desire, and so liberation*
> *From the future as well as the past. Thus, love of a country*
> *Begins as attachment to our own field of action*
> *And comes to find that action of little importance*
> *Though never indifferent. History may be servitude,*
> *History may be freedom.*

Each writer looked for the history which is freedom; each found, to a lesser or greater extent, the history which is servitude. Pound was trapped in his ruined house of documents; Yeats turned on the Great Wheel of Recurrence. Adams was an ironic cheerleader, urging history toward its explosive conclusion. Malraux experimented with ideology and opted for action; he stood too close to History to see her plain. Eliot and Mann, traveling the painful road of mediation, discovered that history "is what it always was": the knowledge of human defeat and partial victory; the process which periodically runs out of control. But our writers rescued something for eternity. Their work is now part of human memory and helps to liberate us from past and future. Each poem, each novel has passed into literary tradition and hence into the higher historical process: "that pattern of timeless moments" which transcends the violence and horror of our quotidian immediacy.

Notes

CHAPTER I
The Meaning of History, What History *Means*

1. Arthur O. Lovejoy, *The Great Chain of Being* (Cambridge, Mass., 1936), p. 7.

2. Some idea of the range of meaning implied by the term "historicism" may be seen in the two following examples.

In the days of the Weimar Republic, the social philosopher Karl Mannheim named historicism the *Weltanschauung* for the modern age: "Historicism is therefore neither a mere fad nor a fashion; it is not even an intellectual current, but the very basis on which we construct our observations of the socio-cultural reality. It is not something artificially contrived, something like a programme, but an organically developed basic pattern, the *Weltanschauung* itself, which came into being after the religiously determined medieval picture of the world had disintegrated and when the subsequent Enlightenment, with its dominant idea of a supra-temporal Reason, had destroyed itself." From *Essays On the Sociology of Knowledge* (New York, 1952), pp. 84–85.

Erich Auerbach uses the term "historism" (his Englishing of the German *Historismus*) to name nothing as far-reaching and grandiloquent as *Weltanschauung*. Historism is "an acquisition of the human mind . . ." embodied in the belief ". . . that every civilization and every period has its own possibilities of aesthetic perfection; that works of art of the different peoples and periods, as well as their general forms of life, must be understood as products of variable individual conditions, and have to be judged each by its own development, not by absolute rules of beauty and ugliness. General and aesthetic historism is a pre-

191

cious (and also a very dangerous) acquisition of the human mind; it is a comparatively recent one." From *Scenes from the Drama of European Literature* (New York, 1959), pp. 183–184.

3. *Vom Nutzen und Nachteil der Historie für das Leben,* in the German text published by Carl Hanser Verlag (Munich, 1960) and edited by Karl Schlechta. Volume I, p. 210. The translations from Nietzsche are my own.

4. *Ibid.,* p. 243.

5. *Ibid.,* p. 258.

6. *Ibid.,* pp. 262–263.

7. *The Philosophy of History,* translated by J. Sibree (New York, 1956), pp. 72–73.

8. *Ibid.,* p. 74.

9. Ernst Cassirer, *The Myth of the State* (New York, 1955), p. 330.

10. *Ecce Homo,* "Warum Ich Ein Schicksal Bin," (Hanser Verlag, Vol. II), p. 1153.

11. *Also Sprach Zarathustra* (Hanser Verlag, Vol. II), p. 395.

12. *Ibid.,* p. 394.

13. *Die Fröhliche Wissenschaft* (Hanser Verlag, Vol. II), p. 202.

14. *Die Wille zur Macht* (Stuttgart, 1964), Vol. IX, p. 688.

15. Philip Wheelwright, *The Burning Fountain* (Bloomington, 1968), p. 134.

16. *The Myth and the Powerhouse* (New York, 1965), p. 13 ff.

17. See Frank Kermode's *The Sense of an Ending* (New York, 1967).

CHAPTER II

Henry Adams

1. Adams mentions Nietzsche only once in passing in *The Education,* not at all in the *Letters.*

2. *The Education of Henry Adams* (New York: The Modern Library, 1931), p. 109.

3. *The Education,* p. 4.

4. See Edwin Muir, *Essays on Literature and Society* (Cambridge, Mass., 1965), p. 126.

5. Letter to Elizabeth Cameron, January 13, 1898. *Letters of Henry Adams, 1892–1918.* Edited by W. C. Ford (Boston and New York, 1938), p. 145.

6. See Yvor Winters' *In Defense of Reason* (Denver, 1947), p. 398.

7. *Letters,* to Elizabeth Cameron, July 27, 1896, p. 110.

8. *Letters,* to Elizabeth Cameron, September 5, 1899, p. 238.

9. *The Degradation of the Democratic Dogma* (New York, 1920), p. 127.

10. *Ibid.*, p. 283.
11. *Ibid.*, p. 130.
12. *Letters,* to Charles Milnes Gaskell, June 20, 1895, p. 71.
13. Henry Adams refers to his brother Brooks as "my idiot brother" (with ironic affection, of course) in a letter to Elizabeth Cameron, September 25, 1894. *Letters,* p. 57.
14. *Letters,* to Brooks Adams, June 5, 1895, p. 68.
15. Quoted in Ernest Samuels, *Henry Adams: The Major Phase* (Cambridge, Mass., 1964), p. 554.
16. In *Die Fröhliche Wissenschaft* (Hanser Verlag, Vol. II), pp. 126–128.
17. *The Education*, p. 446.
18. *Ibid.*, p. 445.
19. *Ibid.*, p. 380.
20. *Ibid.*, p. 447.
21. Austin Warren, *The New England Conscience* (Ann Arbor, 1966), p. 178.

CHAPTER III

T. S. Eliot

1. "A Sceptical Patrician," *The Athenaeum*, May 23, 1919. 361–362.
2. In earlier editions of Eliot's poetry, the word *Jew* appears as *jew;* in the last American edition *Collected Poems 1909–1962* (New York, 1963) *Jew* is capitalized.
3. The *Origins of Totalitarianism* (New York, 1951), p. 171.
4. *Ibid.*, p. 112.
5. From an editorial by Eliot (signed "Crites") in *The Criterion*, III, 9 (October 1924), p. 4.
6. Murray Krieger, *A Window to Criticism* (Princeton, 1964).
7. Eliot's note to line 218 of *The Waste Land.*
8. Eliot in *On Poetry and Poets* (New York, 1957), pp. 121–122.
9. George L.K. Morris, "Marie, Marie, Hold on Tight," *Partisan Review*, XXI (March-April 1954), 231–233.

Marie Larisch was Rudolph's first cousin and acted as the intermediary between Rudolph and his teen-age mistress, Mary Vetsera. Rudolph and Mary were found shot to death in the imperial hunting lodge at Mayerling. The usual verdict has been double suicide but the matter has never been satisfactorily cleared up.
10. *The Philosophy of History* (edition cited), p. 103.

11. From Hesse's *Blick ins Chaos* (1920). Translation is my own. See "The Downfall of Europe," *Western Review*, XVII (Spring 1953), 185–195.

12. Reinhold Niebuhr, *The Nature and Destiny of Man*, Volume II, *Human Destiny* (New York: The Scribner Library, 1964; first published, 1943), p. 299.

13. *The Myth and the Powerhouse*, p. 15.

CHAPTER IV

W. B. Yeats

1. *A Vision* (New York: Macmillan Paperbacks, 1961. Reissue of revised edition of 1956.), p. 299.

2. Mircea Eliade, *The Quest: History and Meaning in Religion* (Chicago, 1969), p. 48.

3. Nietzsche, "Vom Nutzen und Nachteil," edition cited.

4. Hazard Adams, "Yeats, Dialectic, and Criticism," *Criticism*, X, 3 (Summer, 1968), 185.

5. Conor Cruise O'Brien, "Passion and Cunning: an Essay on the Politics of W.B. Yeats," in *Excited Reverie* (New York, 1965), p. 276.

6. See *The City of God*, Book XI, Chapter XIII, Temple Classics Edition (London and Toronto, 1931), Part Two, p. 242.

7. Heraclitus, fragment 18. In Philip Wheelwright's *Heraclitus* (New York: Atheneum Paperback, 1964), p. 20.

8. Heraclitus, fragment 66 (edition cited), p. 68.

9. *A Vision*, p. 68.

10. *Ibid.*, p. 250.

11. *Ibid.*, p. 257.

12. *Ibid.*, p. 257.

13. *Ibid.*, p. 262.

14. *Ibid.*, p. 302.

15. *Civilization and Its Discontents*, translated by James Strachey (New York, 1961), p. 92.

16. See Norman Cohn's *The Pursuit of the Millennium* (London: Temple Smith, 1970). On Joachim of Flora (or Fiore), see pp. 108–110; on Jan Bockelson and the "Münster revolutionaries," see pp. 267–280.

17. *The Philosophy of History* (edition cited), p. 23.

18. *Ibid.*, p. 15.

19. *The Phenomenology of Mind*, translated by J.B. Baillie (London and New York, 1949, 1961), p. 549.

20. *Ibid.*, p. 517.
21. Erich Heller, "Yeats and Nietzsche," *Encounter* XXXIII, 6 (December 1969), p. 64.
22. *Ibid.*, p. 72.
23. Philip Rieff, *The Triumph of the Therapeutic* (New York and Evanston: Harper Torchbooks, 1968), p. 2.

CHAPTER V
The Cantos *of Ezra Pound*

1. Hugh Kenner, *The Poetry of Ezra Pound* (London, 1951).
2. The *Cantos* appear variously numbered in different editions, some with Roman, others with Arabic numerals. For simplicity I use Arabic numerals throughout.
3. See Carl Van Doren's *Benjamin Franklin* (New York, 1938), p. 745 and note on p. 806.
4. *The Spirit of Romance* (2nd edition, Norfolk, Conn., 1952), p. 8.
5. Ernst Cassirer, *The Philosophy of the Enlightenment* (Princeton, 1951), p. 204.
6. From Gobineau, quoted in Hannah Arendt's *The Origins of Totalitarianism*, p. 171.
7. *Ibid.*, p. 325.
8. Daniel D. Pearlman, *The Barb of Time* (New York, 1969), pp. 209–210.

CHAPTER VI
André Malraux

1. See the *Anti-Memoirs,* translated by Terence Kilmartin (New York, 1968), p. 207: ". . . I had never been a member of the Communist Party or of the International Brigade . . ."
2. Leon Trotsky, "The Strangled Revolution," in *Malraux,* edited by R.W.B. Lewis (Englewood Cliffs, N.J., 1964), p. 15. For Malraux's reply to Trotsky, see p. 21.
3. See Malraux's *Postface* to *The Conquerors* (Boston, 1956), p. 175.
4. Karl Marx, from *The Holy Family* (1845). Reprinted in *Selected Writings in Sociology and Social Philosophy,* translated by T.B. Bottomore (London and New York, 1956, 1964), p. 63.
5. I am indebted to Irving Howe for the Ch'en-Kirilov parallels. See *Politics and the Novel* (New York, 1957), p. 214.
6. Oswald Spengler, *Der Untergang des Abendlandes,* Vol. II, *Welthistorische Perspektiven* (Munich, 1922), p. 635.

7. See R.G. Collingwood, *Essays in the Philosophy of History* (New York: McGraw Hill Paperbacks, 1966), p. 71.
8. *Anti-Memoirs,* p. 9.
9. *Ibid.,* p. 8.
10. See, for example, "Noon" in *Zarathustra* (part IV) and the "Nachgesang" in *Beyond Good and Evil.*

CHAPTER VII
Thomas Mann

1. "At the Prophet's," in *Stories of Three Decades,* translated by H.T. Lowe-Porter (New York, 1936), p. 288.
2. In a letter to Kurt Martens (June 13, 1904) Mann remarks, "In 'At the Prophet's' I have depicted the self-possession of Frau Prof. P. and cannot believe that she will be angry with me over that inoffensive homage." See *Thomas Mann: Briefe 1889–1936,* edited by Erika Mann (S. Fischer Verlag, 1962), p. 48.
3. See Mann's letter to his brother Viktor (February 20, 1948): "Zur Höhe is rather Derleth, not George." *Briefe 1948–1955* (Frankfurt am Main, 1965), p. 23.
4. "Nietzsche's Philosophy in the Light of Contemporary Events," in *Thomas Mann's Addresses* (Washington, D.C.: Library of Congress, 1963), p. 100.
5. *Doctor Faustus,* translated by H.T. Lowe-Porter (New York, 1948), p. 368.
6. *Ibid.,* p. 371.
7. "A Brother," translated by H.T. Lowe-Porter, in *Order of the Day* (New York, 1942), p. 157.
8. *Civilization and its Discontents,* translated by James Strachey (edition cited), p. 59.
9. *Ibid.,* p. 77.
10. *Ibid.,* p. 92.
11. "Death in Venice," in *Stories of Three Decades,* p. 412.
12. *Ibid.,* p. 384.
13. I echo here one of Herbert Marcuse's most frequently quoted *dicta:* "Psychological problems therefore turn into political problems; private disorder reflects more directly than before the disorder of the whole . . ." From *Eros and Civilization* (New York: Vintage Books, n.d.), p. xvii.
14. "A Brother," in *Order of the Day,* p. 154.
15. *Jenseits von Gut und Böse (Beyond Good and Evil),* Schlechta, Vol. II, pp. 705–706. The translation is my own.

16. See Harvey Gross's "Reopening the Case of Wagner," *The American Scholar*, 38, 1 (Winter 1968–69), p. 120.
17. Michael Hamburger, *Contraries* (New York, 1970), p. 264.
18. See *Der Fall Wagner* (*The Case of Wagner*), Schlechta, Vol. II, p. 904. "Durch Wagner redet die Modernität ihre *intimste* Sprache . . . Wagner resümiert die Modernität." ("Through Wagner modernity speaks its *most intimate* language . . . Wagner sums up modernity.")
19. "The German Republic," translated by H.T. Lowe-Porter, in *Order of the Day*, p. 44.
20. *The Magic Mountain*, translated by H.T. Lowe-Porter (New York, 1927), p. 343.
21. *Ibid.*, p. 347.
22. *Ibid.*, p. 400.
23. *Ibid.*, p. 709.
24. *Ibid.*, p. 495.
25. What elements of critique Mann omits in *Doctor Faustus* itself, he includes in its fascinating *parergon, Die Entstehung des Doktor Faustus* (*The Story of a Novel*).
26. *Doctor Faustus*, p. 375.
27. *Ibid.*, p. 243.
28. From the apocryphal Old Testament IV Ezra, 5:55. Quoted in Martin Buber's *On the Bible: Eighteen Studies* (New York, 1968), p. 183. I am indebted to Buber for the important distinction between "biblical prophetic" and "biblical apocalyptic."
29. *On the Bible*, p. 183.
30. *Ibid.*, p. 174.

AFTERWORD

1. W.H. Auden, *Collected Shorter Poems 1927–1957* (New York: Random House, 1966), p. 15.
2. Karl Marx and Friedrich Engels, *Correspondence 1846–1895*, tr. Dona Torr (New York, 1935), p. 91.
3. Arthur O. Lovejoy, *The Great Chain of Being* (Cambridge, Mass., 1936), p. 12.
4. Thomas Mann, *Past Masters* (New York, 1933), p. 177.
5. I paraphrase here some unpublished remarks Eliot made in 1933. See F.O. Matthiessen's *The Achievement of T.S. Eliot* (Boston and New York, 1935), pp. 89–90 and p. 96.

Index

Adams, Brooks, 193; *The Law of Civilization and Decay,* 25.
Adams, Hazard, 78, 194.
Adams, Henry, 20–31; *The Degradation of the Democratic Dogma,* 23; "A Letter to American Teachers of History," 24; *Mont-Saint-Michel and Chartres,* 22; "The Rule of Phase Applied to History," 24.
Adams, John, 107.
Aquinas, Thomas, 151.
Amor fati, 16, 42, 90, 94, 127.
Anti-Semitism, 21, 41, 42, 114.
Apocalypse, 7, 16, 70, 92, 137.
Arendt, Hannah, xii, 41, 121, 193.
Auden, W. H., 99, 163, 185–86.
Auerbach, Erich, 191.
Augustine, St., 15; *The City of God,* 74.

Bayle, Pierre, 109.
Beethoven, Ludwig van, 64, 111, 180.
Berenson, Bernard, 25.
Bergson, Henri, 26.
Bockelson, Jan, 87.
Brahms, Johannes, 168, 180.

Browne, Sir Thomas, 167.
Buber, Martin, 1, 184, 197.
Burke, Kenneth, 161.

Cameron, Elizabeth, 21.
Carlyle, Thomas, 2, 21, 30.
Cassirer, Ernst, 10, 109, 192.
Charles I (King of England), 70.
Chou En-lai, 125.
Churchill, Winston, 108–9.
Cohn, Norman, 194.
Collingwood, R. G., 146, 196.
Confucius, 121.

Dante, 33, 101, 119, 178–79.
Derleth, Ludwig, 121.
Diaghilev, Sergei, 171.
Donne, John, 65.
Dostoevsky, Fyodor, 57, 135–36.
Dreyfus Affair, 21, 42.

Einstein, Albert, 121–22.
Eliade, Mircea, 194.
Eliot, T. S., 32–73; *Four Quartets,* 58–72; *Gerontion,* 32–44; *The Hollow Men,* 8; *The Idea of a Christian Society,* 61; *The Waste Land,* 44–58, 171.

Emerson, Ralph Waldo, 61, 76.
Empson, William, 138.
Eschaton, 2, 16, 152.
Eternal Recurrence, 13, 39, 67, 78, 81, 91–92, 94.

Fiedler, Leslie, 27.
FitzGerald, Edward, 34.
Ford, Henry, 123.
Franklin, Benjamin, 107.
Franz Josef, 51.
Frazer, J. G., 49, 84.
Frederick the Great, 166.
Freud, Sigmund, 26, 86, 89, 122; *Civilization and Its Discontents*, 161–63.

Gaskell, Charles Milnes, 25, 41.
Gaulle, Charles de, 125.
George, Stefan, 121, 196.
Gobineau, Joseph-Arthur de, 111, 114.

Hamburger, Michael, 197.
Hegel, G. W. F., 14, 30, 40, 56, 89, 102, 145, 151, 188; *The Phenomenology of Mind*, 96; *The Philosophy of History*, 7–10, 14, 32, 49, 92–93.
Heller, Erich, 97, 168, 195.
Hemingway, Ernest, 28, 171.
Heraclitus, 67, 74, 82.
Herodotus, 2.
Hesse, Hermann, 57, 85; *Blick ins Chaos*, 194.
Hitler, Adolf, 125, 181.
Historicism, 6–7, 191–92.
Howe, Irving, 195.

Isaiah, 73.

Jaspers, Karl, 185.

Jefferson, Thomas, 121.
Joachim of Flora, 86.
John, Saint (the Evangelist), 63.
Johnson, Samuel, 100.
Joyce, James, 15, 171.

Kenner, Hugh, 101.
Kermode, Frank, xii, 16.
Khrushchev, Nikita, 11.
Krieger, Murray, 45.
Kuomintang, 129.

Larisch, Marie, 51.
Lawrence, D. H., 27, 28.
Leopold, Duke, 106.
Litvinof, Maxim, 107.
Lovejoy, Arthur, 186, 191.
Löwith, Karl, xi.
Lucretius, 27.
Ludwig II (King of Bavaria), 50.
Luther, Martin, 182–83.

Mahler, Gustav, 180.
Malraux, André, 124–54; *Anti-Memoirs*, 124, 125, 147; *The Conquerors*, 125–29; *Man's Fate*, 129–36; *Man's Hope*, 136–42; *The Temptation of the West*, 142–45; *The Walnut Trees of Altenburg*, 146–54.
Mann, Thomas, 155–84; "At the Prophet's, 156–58; "Blood of the Walsungs," 170; "Bruder Hitler," 160–61; *Buddenbrooks*, 155, 158; *Death in Venice*, 164–67; *Doctor Faustus*, 158–59, 178–84; *Fiorenza*, 106; "Gladius Dei," 155, 160; *The Magic Mountain*, 167–78; *The Story of a Novel*, 155; *Tristan*, 170.
Mannheim, Karl, 142, 191.

Mannin, Ethel, 80.
Marcuse, Herbert, 196.
Marinetti, Emilio, 171.
Martov, Julius, 11.
Marx, Karl, 16, 92, 115, 120, 130.
Matthiessen, F. O., 197.
Maurras, Charles, 42, 60.
Merwin, W. S., 161.
Middleton, Thomas, 40.
Milton, John, 70, 119.
Morris, George L. K., 50, 193.
Muir, Edwin, 21, 192.
Mussolini, Benito, 121, 125.

Niebuhr, Reinhold, 63, 194.
Nietzsche, Friedrich, 10, 11–14, 20, 26, 30, 71, 75–76, 97, 99, 127, 144, 149–50, 153, 169, 188; *The Birth of Tragedy*, 35; *The Gay Science (Die Fröhliche Wissenschaft)*, 13, 26; "Of the Use and Disadvantage of History for Life" (*Vom Nutzen und Nachteil der Historie für das Leben*), 7–9, 192; *Thus Spake Zarathustra*, 14.
Nordau, Max, 25.
Novus dux, 86–87.

O'Brien, Conor Cruise, 80, 194.
O'Duffy, General Eoin, 87.

Pearlman, Daniel D., 121–22.
Perse, St.-J. (Alexis St. Leger), 142.
Plato, 150.
Pound, Ezra, 100–123; 19, 48, 171; *Drafts & Fragments of Cantos CX–CXVII*, 102; *Section: Rock Drill*, 100, 102; *The Spirit of Romance*, 107; *Thrones*, 102.

Pringsheim, Hedwig, 157.
Rahv, Philip, 15, 72.
Ranke, Leopold von, 14.
Reichenbach, Hans, 168.
Rieff, Philip, 98.
Rilke, Rainer Maria, 171.
Rudolph, Archduke, 51.

Samuels, Ernest, 193.
Schacht, Hjalmar, 106.
Schönberg, Arnold, 171, 180.
Shelley, Percy Bysshe, 119, 186.
Socrates, 165.
Sorel, Georges, 26.
Spengler, Oswald, 14, 21, 30, 56, 143, 145, 146, 148–49, 176, 195.
Stalin, Joseph, 126.

Theodicy, 11, 59, 92–93.
Toller, Ernst, 80.
Toynbee, Arnold, 14.
Trotsky, Leon, 11, 125–26, 195; *History of the Russian Revolution*, 15.

Unamuno, Miguel de, 140.

Verlaine, Paul, 51.
Vetsera, Mary, 51.
Vico, Giambattista, 15, 77.
Virgil, 146.

Wagner, Richard, 50, 101, 115, 168, 169, 180; *Parsifal*, 51; *Das Rheingold*, 51, 54; *Tristan und Isolde*, 51.
Warren, Austin, 29, 116, 193.
Warren, Robert Penn, 1–6.
Weston, Jesse, 49.
Wheelwright, Philip, 15, 82, 192.
Winters, Yvor, 22, 192.
Wordsworth, William, 46.

Yeats, William Butler, 74–99; "Byzantium," 87–89; "The Great Day," 87; "The Gyres," 89–91; "Leda and the Swan," 79; "Meru," 95–96; "The Magi," 77–79; "News for the Delphic Oracle," 89; *The Resurrection*, 82–86, 95; "The Second Coming," 77, 80–82; "The Valley of the Black Pig," 79; *A Vision*, 75, 77, 82, 85; *The Wanderings of Oisin*, 97.

Zaharoff, Basil, 113.
Zola, Emile, 21.